the series on school reform

Patricia A. Wasley
University of Washington

Ann Lieberman
NCREST

Joseph P. McDonald
New York University

SERIES EDITORS

(Continued)

INSIDE THE NATIONAL WRITING PROJECT

Connecting Network Learning and Classroom Teaching

ANN LIEBERMAN AND DIANE R. WOOD

Teachers College, Columbia University
New York and London

Published by Teachers College Press, 1234 Amsterdam Avenue, New York, NY 10027

Copyright © 2003 by Teachers College, Columbia University

Library of Congress Cataloging-in-Publication Data

Lieberman, Ann.
    Inside the National Writing Project : connecting network learning and classroom teaching / Ann Lieberman and Diane R. Wood.
        p. cm. -- (The series on school reform)
    Includes bibliographical references and index.
    ISBN 0-8077-4301-1 (pbk. : alk.paper) -- ISBN 0-8077-4302-X (cloth : alk. paper)
        1. English teachers--Training of--California--Berkeley. 2. English language--Rhetoric--Study and teaching--California--Berkeley.
    3. Report writing--Study and teaching (Higher)--California--Berkeley.
    4. National Writing Project (U.S.). I. Wood, Diane (Diane R.) II. Title.
    III. Series.
PE1405.U6 L54   2003
428'.0071'179467--dc21   2002031953

ISBN 0-8077-4301-1 (paper)
ISBN 0-8077-4302-X (cloth)

Printed on acid-free paper
Manufactured in the United States of America

10 09 08 07 06 05 04 03   8 7 6 5 4 3 2 1

Contents

Preface

We both knew of the National Writing Project (NWP) but little of its details. We knew that teachers talked fondly about it but wondered what it was that attracted so many teachers to this professional development project. Having studied school reform networks, we became interested in studying the NWP as a professional development project in a network context. We simultaneously met with members of the national staff and sought funding to do a study in two sites. In this way each of us could develop an in-depth relationship to our site and could get inside the network. We opted for depth rather than breadth.

After several meetings with the NWP staff, trying to decide which two sites we would study, we decided that Ann would study the UCLA writing project, an older site. Diane would travel to Oklahoma to study a younger site, combining a rural, suburban, and urban context. We thought that doing so would not only give us different contexts but also help us understand what sites did similarly and what they did that helped them accommodate to or negotiate the context.

April 27, 1998. I (Ann) made my second visit to UCLA. I was to meet a group of teachers and introduce the study we were about to begin. I walked into Moore Hall, a building I had been in many times. In a beautiful large room with high ceilings and large windows on the second floor, 10 teachers and the director and co-director of the UCLA writing project were seated around a huge table. I was nervous, wondering if I could say explicitly what our study was about and why we thought it was important to do. There were cookies and drinks in the back of the room, welcoming the teachers to this after-school meeting. The director introduced me: "Ann Lieberman is here to tell you about a study that she and

Diane Wood are doing in two sites of the Writing Project".

It was my turn to talk. I began talking quickly, hoping to connect our interests to their lives and concerns. "For years we have heard about how teachers say that they have been transformed by the Writing Project. We want to find out what they mean. What is it that happens to people during the five-week invitational? And how is this work followed up by the local site?"

That is all I said. I wanted to explain what we would do, whom we would interview, how we would hold focus groups, how we would go to classrooms, how we would follow six teachers. I also wanted to say that no one to date had investigated whether network learning actually found its way into the classroom. But the room erupted with teachers talking excitedly and passionately.

- "The writing project changed my life."
- "It gave me a community of teachers who cared passionately about constantly improving their practice."
- "I have continued to learn about my own teaching and now I am called upon by my colleagues to teach them."
- "We have tackled the toughest problems of urban teaching here and found many colleagues willing to engage in the struggle."
- "I was a new teacher when I first went to the Invitational. It not only kept me in teaching, but I learned what it meant to be a real professional, to inquire, to ask questions."

And so it went for 2 more hours. At six o'clock, no one got up to go home. The study had officially begun . . .

Acknowledgments

In all efforts such as this one, there are many people to be acknowledged. First and foremost, Richard Sterling and Elyse Aidman-Ahdahl not only spent a lot of time listening to us describe our study but also helped us think about our work in much more expansive terms. Bill Hawley, director of the National Partnership for Excellence and Accountability (NPEAT), supported us by a generous grant during 1998–2000. Gary Griffin, an old and good friend, helped us conceptualize this study so that it not only got funded but also had the potential for making a contribution to our understanding of networks—and their connections to teacher and student learning. Sarah Freedman helped us in so many ways to understand the NWP and to dig deeply into its complexities.

Joye Alberts and Faye Peitzman, co-directors from Oklahoma State University (OSU) and the University of California at Los Angeles (UCLA), respectively, became good friends, guiding us through their "sites"—spending enormous amounts of time to help us see the depth and breadth of their sites. And they continue to give us feedback in classic NWP fashion. Mary Belvin, Marlene Carter, Laura Jacobs, Sidonie Myrick, Linda Thomas, and Lisa Ummel-Ingram—the six teachers we studied—were amazingly flexible and generous in letting us into their classrooms. We asked them endless questions in person and by email, trying to understand the connections between what they were learning and how it showed up in their classroom practice.

During October of 2000, we received a fellowship from the Rockefeller Foundation to go to Bellagio, Italy, to write this book. We figured out what we wanted to write and got a great start on the book, but, more importantly, we made friends with an extraordinary group of people from all over the world doing wonderful work to better humankind. We gained greater clarity when we took our turn telling about our study to scientists, sculptors, poets, mathematicians, sociologists, medical researchers, and nonprofit administrators.

Joe Wood encouraged and supported us, engaging with the ideas of this book, and reading excerpts along the way. Ernie Lieberman was a wonderful editor and critic, helping us untangle complicated ideas so that they were not only readable but also well thought out and clearly stated. Both Joe and Ernie have been there for us despite our being consumed with this book for more than 3 years.

Ruby Kerawalla helped us put this book together by correcting references and seeing that chapters were all there. Her technological prowess is outdone only by her good humor and decency.

We were honored that focus groups of teachers at both sites came to talk with us and let us into their culture—one that we hope gets the kind of recognition it deserves.

CHAPTER 1

Developing a Network for Teacher Learning and Professional Development

The respect for teacher knowledge is genuine. It is the heart of it and the whole force behind what we do.
(Site Director, UCLA, Interview, 1998)

Because of the NWP, I am constantly learning. . . . It's not just a one-time workshop. I value my learning and my colleagues' learning. And that growth process that we all go through is so obvious in such a short time in the NWP. You watch it in the summer institute and then after it takes on a whole new life. You keep seeing people grow.
(Teacher, Oklahoma State University site, Interview, 1999)

It has been more than a century since the beginning of public education in the United States, and every decade since has seen efforts to change, improve, or reform schools. From the "efficiency" movement in the 1920s to the Great Society programs in the 1970s, from the "reform era" of the 1980s to the 1990s, emphasis on standards and testing along with different movements and policies have come and gone. With a few exceptions, however, federal, state, and local programs have been unable to affect how schools are organized, how teachers teach, and the substance of what students learn.

While we have learned much about the complexity of school cultures, the difficulty of implementing new ideas, and the layered contexts that confound school-improvement efforts (Fullan, 2001; McDonald et al., 1999), it is only in the last two decades that attention has been paid to the role of teachers as primary actors in schools and school reform efforts. Research showing how teachers develop pedagogical knowledge and the contexts that support this development (Cochran-Smith & Lytle, 1993; Grossman, Wineburg, & Woolworth, 2000; Hargreaves, 1994; Lieberman, 1996; McLaughlin & Talbert, 1993) is changing the way we think about both policy and practice. Darling-Hammond (1998) has provided a basis for suggesting

> a different approach to producing, sharing, and using knowledge, a different paradigm for educational policymaking, one in which policymakers shift their efforts from *designing controls* intended to direct the system to *developing capacity* that enables schools and teachers to be responsible for student learning and responsive to diverse and changing student and community needs. (p. 643, emphasis added)

This approach further suggests that policies encouraging the professional development of teachers be informed by the necessity to do the following:

- Support organizations that enable teachers to become members of professional communities (McLaughlin, 1998)
- Understand the importance of local knowledge and the specific nature of solutions to problems and practices that occur in particular contexts (Cochran-Smith & Lytle, 1990)
- Recognize that both "inside" knowledge (created by teachers) and "outside" knowledge (created by reformers, researchers, and so forth) are valuable and deserving of respect (Lieberman & Miller, 1999)

THE ROLE OF TEACHERS IN PROFESSIONAL DEVELOPMENT

The history of professional development for teachers is a landscape littered with failed approaches. While the names have changed over the years—from "in-service education" to "staff development" to "professional development"—the forms and substance have remained virtually the same.

Teachers have been considered passive consumers of prepackaged knowledge or, at best, compliant participants whose role has been to absorb information from the research and reform communities—whether or not it is useful or appropriate (Cochran-Smith & Lytle, 1999; Little, 1993). As teachers have known and research has shown, "professional development" of teachers has been notoriously unsuccessful. In fact, although large sums of money have been spent by states and districts on professional development, there is little knowledge about how, or even if, professional development organized for teachers ever finds its way into classrooms to enlarge teachers' repertoires and enhance student learning. School districts have often organized professional development opportunities without regard to their teachers' perceived needs or the daily classroom dilemmas they face. Experts who are hired to provide staff development opportunities rarely understand the specific contexts of the teachers that they are supposed to be "developing." Knowledge that teachers acquire through experience in their own classrooms is often not seen as a legitimate guide for improving classroom practice, while differences among teachers in terms of experience, age, or context are largely ignored or glossed over. Moreover, learning opportunities for teachers rarely consider conceptions of change that involve the participation of teachers themselves and the necessity for follow-up and support over time (Fullan & Hargreaves, 1996). Professional development is most often presented as a series of workshops, with rare provisions for trying out the ideas in one's classroom and working on them long enough to internalize them. Teachers are "in-serviced," as if teaching were merely a set of technical skills that could be memorized and applied in all times and places. In the face of these traditional approaches to professional development, it is not surprising that improvements in schools have been minimal and that teachers have grown weary of efforts to "develop" them.

EDUCATIONAL REFORM AND
PROFESSIONAL DEVELOPMENT NETWORKS

In contrast to—or perhaps because of—this history of failure to improve teaching through the traditional approaches to professional development, a new approach, involving teachers as primary actors in their own development, has become increasingly significant. Unlike professional development strategies that have a "one size fits all" orientation, *educational reform networks* provide opportunities for teachers to commit themselves, in small and large ways, to topics that are of interest to them or that arise out of their work. In addition to formal learning, by participating in informal groups they develop stronger voices to represent their perspectives, learn to exercise leadership among their peers, and, perhaps most important, develop a community of shared understanding. These learning communities help them to enrich their teaching while providing the intellectual and emotional support necessary for personal and enduring growth and development (Lieberman & McLaughlin, 1992).

In important ways educational reform and professional development networks and partnerships appear to be uniquely adapted to the rapid technological and socioeconomic changes taking place in American society.

These loose, borderless, flexible organizations can move quickly, inventing new structures and activities as necessary, to respond to the changing needs and concerns of their members. Agendas sensitive to teachers' individual and collective development are supported by cultures that dignify teachers' contributions to pedagogical knowledge as well as to those of the academy.

A study of 16 education reform networks identified some central characteristics that, regardless of their differences of origin and purpose, were shared by all the networks (Lieberman & Grolnick, 1993). These characteristics included the following:

- Agendas more challenging than prescriptive
- Learning more indirect than direct
- Formats more collaborative than individualistic
- Work more integrated than fragmented

- Leadership more facilitative than directive
- Thinking that encouraged multiple rather than unitary perspectives
- Values that were both context-specific and generalized
- Structures that were more movement-like than organization-like.

These characteristics, when integrated into a coherent network or partnership structure, created improvement opportunities for teacher growth that were in marked contrast to traditional professional development or reform models. However, while many of the teachers studied stated that their experiences in these networks had been "transforming," there was little or no information about what these transformative experiences were, how they translated into teachers' classroom practice, and what, if any, effects they had on student learning and accomplishment.

As educational networks become a larger and more influential part of the reform landscape, it is increasingly important to understand them organizationally as well as to understand their work, their influence, and their effects on both teachers and students. Since the National Writing Project (NWP) is arguably the most successful educational network in the history of American education, we recognized that understanding how it works and why it continues to grow in members, sites, and influence can help in dealing with the vexing problem of professional development for teachers. But the first step is finding out how the NWP had come to be. Where did the ideas come from, and how did they take root and grow?

THE NATIONAL WRITING PROJECT:
ITS EVOLUTION AND DEVELOPMENT

The National Writing Project evolved from the struggles of a young teacher to understand how to teach literature and composition to classes of teenagers. Jim Gray, the founder of the original Bay Area Writing Project in 1974, had been a secondary English teacher who taught from the classical literature texts. Disappointed with the standard "three-poems-per-poet" approach, he began to experiment. Gray made his classroom into a library: creating book lists, finding books that would interest his students, and giving "book talks" to engage them. Students began to care about books and to read and discuss them. This approach to reading—encouraging students to read freely and providing them with time to talk with their peers—began to sow the seeds of Gray's learning as a teacher. Eventually, this participatory approach found its way into what was to become "the Writing Project." (For a more detailed description of the origins of the Writing Project, see Gray, 2000.)

In the process of changing their practice, Gray and his colleagues at San Leandro High School began to rebel against the standard professional development efforts at their school. Experts from the outside were going to be called in to create a new English curriculum. Gray and several of his colleagues began asking why the teachers themselves couldn't create a curriculum. Why was it that teachers' knowledge and experience weren't important in any discussion of how to improve the curriculum?

If teachers had developed a strategy or an effective way of working with their students that was producing good results, it seemed reasonable that they should have a way of sharing these ideas with their peers. Gray and his colleagues, from their own experience, knew that teachers made many excellent innovations in the process of teaching their own students, but there were few, if any, organized ways for teachers to learn from one another. What was needed was to develop some opportunities for teachers to teach teachers. Crucial to this seemingly simple idea was the understanding that teachers now had to become the learners—learning from other teachers as well as teaching them. Teachers had to become readers and writers themselves, experience what their students experienced, in order to become sensitive to their own teaching. This seemingly simple yet difficult and complex idea became the bedrock upon which the Writing Project was built.

During the 1970s, amid a deluge of books and articles lamenting "Why Johnny Can't Write," there was much concern that students were coming to colleges and universities not knowing how to write. The time was ripe for innovation. By the summer of 1974, Gray, who had been a supervisor of student teachers for 13 years at the University of California at Berkeley, proposed and received support for starting a Bay Area Summer Institute for the teaching of writing.

Twenty-nine teachers came together to start what was to become an extraordinary professional development effort. The institute, held on the Berkeley campus, represented a new way of thinking about relationships with teachers. It was to be a partnership between the university and a group of local teachers proceeding from the central idea that a university-based organization could dignify the proposition that *teacher knowledge was to be the starting point for learning*. This, joined with several other propositions, continued to be central principles for the Writing Project:

- A "site" is a group of local teachers in partnership with a university or college.
- Teachers teach one another their "best practices."
- Teachers write and present their own work.
- Teachers read, discuss, and analyze research, reforms, and other literature.

Shaped and nuanced over the years, these principles have become the commonly agreed-upon core of the National Writing Project, tying together its many "sites" and laying the foundation for an expanding national organization.[1]

The beginning Bay Area Writing Project attracted immediate attention, becoming the springboard for an eventual statewide network of 18 sites in California that has grown, as of this writing, to 175 sites in all 50 states, Washington, D.C., and Puerto Rico. Through 1998, the NWP had served over 2 million teachers and

---

[1] A site grows out of a university–school partnership. The university is the contractual agent and "owner" of the site. Beginning sites receive $25,000 and must document both their plans and the actual work they do as well as the nature of their continuing work throughout the year. There are smaller targeted grants for specific activities such as Teacher Inquiry, Project Outreach, and Rural Sites.

181,402 administrators (NWP, 1999), with currently more than 12,921 NWP teacher consultants conducting programs for their colleagues throughout the country (NWP, 2000).

As the NWP took its program to a national arena, participants delineated three crucial phases of its mission: to improve the teaching of writing in schools; to provide professional development opportunities for classroom teachers; and to expand the professional roles of teachers. Congruent with this mission, the NWP developed a set of principles to guide its ongoing and expanding work:

- Universities and schools are better able to improve students' learning if they work in a partnership.
- Teachers are key to educational reform.
- Teachers are the best teachers of other teachers.
- Writing deserves constant attention from kindergarten to the university.
- Exemplary teachers of writing are themselves writers (NWP, 2000).

These principles are now embedded in every site's yearly 5-week summer institute, which initiates new members into each local site. In addition, the same principles guide professional development work that NWP teachers design for colleagues in their buildings, districts, and beyond.

A recent study of the NWP has found that when teachers responded a year after they had taken the summer invitational institute, they had gained valuable knowledge and skills; furthermore, they had changed their practices in their classrooms as well (St. John, Dickey, Hirabayashi, & Stokes, 2001). In addition, the Academy for Educational Development (AED), is currently conducting a 3-year study to collect data on how student writing is developed in classrooms, the conditions that support student achievement in writing, and the outcomes for students in NWP classrooms (Fancsali & Nelsestuen, 2001). More details about these research studies are presented in Chapter 5.

WHAT WE WANTED TO KNOW

We came to this study of the NWP convinced that there was something about the NWP that made it popular with teachers, but we knew little about how it was organized, how teachers got involved, or the nature of what they learned. But we knew that we had to get inside the NWP, to see it in action, to learn about its effects on teachers: how they worked with colleagues and how they practiced their craft in their classrooms. (For a full description of our study design, see the Appendix.)

Our study, conducted over a 2-year period, had three primary purposes. We wanted to understand "up close" how and in what ways the NWP facilitates teacher learning in the context of a professional community. We wanted to find out what (if anything) teachers take back to their schools and classrooms from their summer participation and how (or if) these teacher learnings affected their classrooms and students. And lastly, we were interested in how each site created its own network arrangements for teachers' ongoing support and professional development. Our questions were very straightforward:

- How do sites enable (or constrain) teacher development and student learning in a network context?
- What are the key attributes of the sites, and how do they provide for technical and intellectual learning and the building of community?
- What strategies are developed to address and respond to the particulars of the local sites?

We set out to document the entire summer program in two different sites, with the focus being the 5-week summer institute, which we were informed was at the heart of the NWP program. We chose to look at two sites in two different states, one urban and one that combined rural, suburban, and urban areas. At the Los Angeles site, the Writing Project is housed at the University of California at Los Angeles (UCLA) within the School of Education's

Center X (a center whose major purpose is to understand where practice and theory meet). This site was more than 20 years old at the time of our study. The Oklahoma site, housed at Oklahoma State University (OSU) in Stillwater, serviced northern Oklahoma and was 7 years old. We wanted to find out whether differences in urban and rural contexts mattered to the work of the NWP as well as to compare how a mature and a younger site organized their work. After documenting the summer programs at both sites, we hoped to see what the connections, if any, were between teachers' learning in this network context, changes in their classroom routines and practices, and how (or if) their expanded repertoire eventually showed up in their students' understanding and accomplishment. We knew that the links between network learning, classroom teaching, and student accomplishment were neither direct, obvious, nor easy to find. By documenting the progression from summer institute to classroom work to network participation, we sought to find out why the teachers themselves considered this kind of professional development so transformative and important to their lives.

Aware that the best learning takes place when people seeking improvement in their own practice are actively involved with others (Rogoff, 1994; Wenger, 1998), we wanted to know and understand how this comes about in the NWP. In what activities do teachers actually participate? How do they get engaged both individually and collectively? What helps to bind them into a community? Observing the 5-week summer institute in our two sites, we saw teachers become involved and committed to their own improvement. We came to understand that they were participants in a set of "social practices" that, taken together, make up the "work" of the NWP. These practices, as an integrated set of individual and collective activities joining the intellectual traditions of teaching reading and writing, began to reveal some of the reasons why the NWP appealed to teachers. What these social practices are, how they are organized, and what they mean to the teachers who participate in them provides the first part of our study, described in Chapter 2. This is followed in Chapter 3 by an analysis of how the networks develop and incorporate these social practices even as they subtlely nuance them to deal with the different demands of the context.

In Chapter 4, we follow six teachers to their classrooms, describing what they learned and how they use their learning with their students and their colleagues. We try to untangle once again how the social practices encompass the intellectual content of writing as a discipline even as they seamlessly provide the processes that organize how the learning takes place. Two of the teachers participating in the summer institute during the summer of 1998 were new to the NWP. Four of the other teachers were still teaching and participating as teacher consultants, having taken the summer institute years before.

Chapter 5 discusses the numerous challenges facing the NWP and describes its major contribution to our understanding of effective professional development in a new key—professional development that joins learning, inquiry, and community in a network context.

CHAPTER 2

The "Model" and the "Work": Creating a Social Context for Learning

In all our encounters with members of the NWP, we invariably heard references to "the model" and "the work" and the importance of being faithful to both while expanding the NWP network. Sometimes, our informants seemed to use the terms interchangeably, but eventually we understood that they had different meanings. Together, however, they clearly connoted for members of the NWP network qualities that defined a characteristic approach to professional development. Predictably, getting to the actual meaning of these core ideas, seemingly so embedded in the NWP culture, proved to be a slippery task.

It was far easier to discover what they were *not*. Neither seemed to refer to a collection of techniques or to an organizational structure. Neither alluded to a codified body of knowledge. Looking at the various contexts for "the model" and "the work" didn't provide many clues either. The model is followed and the work pursued in a wide variety of contexts, including the routines of daily life in classrooms, staff development workshops in schools and district offices, education conferences, summer institutes in universities, and even professional conversations in restaurants or homes. Despite our difficulties in nailing these concepts down, we knew they were crucial to understanding the NWP.

Two comments in particular helped steer us in the right direction. First, Elyse Eidman-Aadahl, NWP co-director, told us that "the work" of the NWP really amounts to the "enactment of a culture" (Interview, 2000). Second, the site directors at both the UCLA and OSU sites commented that, if we really wanted to understand the NWP model, we would have to observe the summer institutes, the annual invitationals to induct new members. As one of them explained, "it all happens there." This advice turned out to be invaluable.

We attended the summer institutes of both sites and watched participants, called fellows, build strong learning communities in a remarkably short time. Gradually, it became clear that the model actually refers to three core activities that frame the fellows' interactions, and the work refers to a pervasive set of social practices characterizing those interactions (Lieberman & Wood, 2002, in press). As Eidman-Aadahl had told us, initiates to the NWP are immersed into specific ways of inquiring and relating to one another during the summer institutes. In the short span of 5 weeks, institute fellows break through the isolation, conventions, and individualism that characterize so many teachers' lives (Cohn & Kottkamp, 1993; Goodlad, 1984; Lieberman & Miller, 1991, 1999; Lortie, 1975) and gain a transformed vision of what it means to be a professional teacher and colleague. Having done so, most leave the summer institute ready to play the role of a Writing Project teacher consultant (TC). That is, they are committed to continuous professional learning and an understanding of the role of teachers teaching other teachers. And because they have had opportunities to clarify and articulate what they believe and demonstrate what they know, they are ready to become consultants in the professional development of other teachers in the "NWP way."

THE "MODEL": THE SUMMER INSTITUTE

Over time, as things happen in my life, I can relate it back to the Writing Project and the institute. The big thing for me was realizing I could write. That was such a revelation for me. And then knowing I could help kids learn to write. . . . When school started after the institute, I started thinking *what can I do to solve some of these problems* [in my school] *and to be helpful and supportive of my colleagues*. It was like the institute was sitting there waiting to come out, and I started looking at the same problems in a whole new way. (OSU TC, Interview, 1998)

The invitational was a magical time. We did all the lessons as if we were students. It became part of the fiber of the day. We practiced. We experienced. We thought about it all. We wrote letters saying how we would use the ideas. Every time I wrote a letter, I was modifying lessons in my class-room. It was a time to be reflective on myself as a person and as a teacher. (UCLA TC, Interview, 1999)

As they make plans for the annual summer institutes, site directors and veteran TCs remain consciously faithful to the highly participatory, teacher-centered design that James Gray, the NWP founder, originally developed. These institutes, sometimes also referred to as the summer invitationals, require careful preparation. During the schoolyear, communications go out to NWP teachers, university professors in education and English, building administrators, district officials, and so forth requesting names of potential attendees. The intent, following Gray's original conception, is to bring together teachers who have built reputations for strong, effective teaching. Occasionally, teachers who work with Writing Project colleagues, or have attended workshops led by a TC, or have heard about the NWP in some other way will inquire about membership, find someone to recommend them, and receive an invitation. Most often, however, active TCs and site directors, always looking for potential candidates, make the overtures to prospective institute fellows. Once a list of prospects is compiled, invitations go out and site directors prepare for pre-institute meetings. These pre-institute sessions, occurring in the spring before the summer institute, constitute a first exposure to the NWP model and help participants start preparing for the actual institute.

Three core activities govern the model (Gray, 2000):

- Creating forums for successful teachers to teach one another
- Engaging teachers in reading and discussing relevant educational literature and research

- Providing opportunities for teachers to write and share their writing in response groups

In the weeks before the institute, fellows prepare a teaching demonstration and a writing sample to share.

Fundamentally democratic, the NWP model builds on the assumptions that teachers have built expertise from experience and that what they know needs to be valued and disseminated. The model creates opportunities for teachers to explore what *they* think they want or need to know in order to become better teachers. Further, the model is based on the idea that teachers who teach writing should be writers themselves. Actual engagement in writing allows them to reflect on the *processes* of writing so they will more deeply understand these processes and be better prepared to teach them. Together, the core activities transform solitary work into public performance. They encourage participants to take an interest in their colleagues' thinking, their challenges, and their practice, and they promote collegial feedback and critique. In short, the institutes have a definite curriculum, shaped both by the expertise of institute fellows and by current knowledge in the field of literacy. This curriculum stresses learning as a *social* phenomenon and teaching as a *collective* responsibility.

The teaching demonstrations, for example, give teachers the opportunity to share a classroom strategy or approach with peers. These presentations, quite obviously, draw on participants' expertise, surfacing the practical wisdom that teachers accrue from working with students. Veteran TCs coach institute fellows in the art of teaching demonstrations, helping them to be "very thoughtful" not only about what they want to present but also about *why* they think it is important (TC, Interview, 1998). After each demonstration, the presenter receives oral comments and/or letters from peers, who describe strengths, offer suggestions, ask questions, or imagine how they might incorporate what they've heard into their own work. Overall, as the demonstrations unfold, fellows recognize collective professional expertise, build knowledge, and rethink and revise their own practices.

The teaching demonstrations we saw in the summer institutes ranged over extensive territory. Fellows presented strategies for engaging students in all sorts of reading and writing activities. They demonstrated ways to embed state-mandated standards in classroom lessons without sacrificing a learner-centered classroom. They showed one another how to encourage literacy in students whose first language is not English, as well as how to teach fine points of grammar, spelling, and punctuation without significantly interrupting the writing process. As the ideas and strategies poured out, we saw an ethic of privacy (Little, 1999; Lortie, 1975) give way to an ethic of "swapping ideas." Pride in collective expertise seemed to overcome stage fright as the weeks progressed and individual voices strengthened.

A similar phenomenon occurred as teachers chose research questions to pursue. They shared their questions with one another in the first week and then made periodic progress reports. Typically, a significant amount of time is given over to library study or web searches. Institute fellows search through articles and books stacked on tables and shelves in their gathering places. As they research, they consult one another both informally and in their writing groups. By the last week, they tend to have become invested in one another's topics and, therefore, listen intently as each fellow reports on what he or she has learned. Perhaps most importantly, this aspect of the institute instills a habit of professional reading. As one teacher consultant put it:

> I would say that one of the things . . . [that] the Writing Project is really responsible for. . . is getting me back into reading educational literature. Because other than my master's degree, I didn't really do much of that in the interim years. You just really lose sight of all that. And you're just so much into student papers and just reading the books the students are reading. . . . [At] the Writing Project, one of the things they do is give you a lot of articles, and the idea here being that your practice is *based* on something. It's not just out of the blue, but it's probably based on a theory or it's based on some research. And that was very important for me, so I learned through the reading, and now I . . . buy the journals myself and do a lot more reading on my own. (Interview, 2000)

Over the 5 weeks, institute fellows produce four written papers. Three can be in any style or genre and on any topic; the fourth is a position paper on an educational topic each teacher chooses to research. Some teachers come to the institutes anxious about sharing their writing publicly with their peers. To ease this stress, every fellow is assigned to a small writing group, and these groups create a more comfortable context for sharing writing and receiving feedback. As one TC told us, "My writing group was the best thing for me about the summer institute; they gave me courage" (Interview, 1998). Another said, "You have to have a safe place to start" (Interview, 1999). By the end of the institute, every teacher has taken the "author's chair," a tradition central to the summer institutes as well as to NWP classrooms because it provides a forum for sharing writing. After a teacher reads a paper aloud from the author's chair, colleagues provide feedback. This feedback, in turn, informs subsequent revisions and then revisions are also shared. As drafts improve over time, fellows see for themselves how public presentation has the power to motivate and produce high-quality work.

These three activities are vital in acquainting teachers with norms of the NWP culture and solidifying relationships within the institute cohorts. But there are other contributing factors. Tables in the room, laden with refreshments and teaching resources, provide nourishment for body and mind and deliver the message that people are cared for in the community. Every day a volunteer reads the log of the previous day's activities, affording an opportunity to relive them. This custom conveys a sense of the routines and rhythms of the institute, highlights the significance of shared experiences in building community, and reveals accumulating insights. Also tucked into a typical day's proceedings are 5-minute "quick-writes" to spark reflection or generate ideas. Sometimes fellows participate in special-interest groups, such as "grade-alike" groups, to delve deeply into issues of mutual concern.

Veteran teacher consultants play an active and visible role in the summer institutes. They share original research, model teaching demonstrations, coach fellows in planning their demonstrations, explain special regional initiatives in which they play an

active part, and generally embody the ideal of continuous professional learning and leadership. Informally, veteran TCs are available to give tips on making presentations, to describe ways they
are bringing NWP to other venues, and, in general, to "show the
ropes" to new inductees about what it means to be a contributing
member of the NWP community. Their presence provides a living
example that the work of the NWP continues after the last day of
the institute.

We found that the summer institutes in both sites—in
Oklahoma and California—provide a wide variety of entry points
to invite teacher engagement, and our interviews revealed that
institute fellows differ in terms of what activities they find most
stimulating. But *all* of the fellows and TCs with whom we talked
agreed that they deeply appreciated having the opportunity to
develop and exercise a strong professional voice and to be respectfully heard and critiqued by a committed professional community. In fact, many said these experiences led to a new professional
identity for them. One TC explained:

> The experience of being in the Writing Project is a morale
> booster. I heard between the lines at the summer institute
> that we are professionals, that we are to be valued. There
> was a forum that gave you an opportunity to talk and be
> heard. It's not like at school when teachers' talking is most-
> ly griping. . . . Teachers can move beyond griping to prob-
> lem solving. . . . I think it's about being treated as a profes-
> sional and being valued for your thoughts and ideas and
> knowing you belong to a professional community.
> (Interview, 1998)

Most fellows leave the institute with the intention of creating
similar learning environments for their students and colleagues.
As one TC put it, "I left saying I'm going to do for students what
the Writing Project did for me" (Interview, 1999). Another told us,
"I went to the summer institute specifically to see how it worked
as a professional development experience; then I tried to create a
similar experience for colleagues in my district" (Interview, 1999).
At the end of the institutes, most fellows choose to become teacher

consultants, or TCs, professionally authorized by the strength of their network's reputation and their own enhanced sense of efficacy to teach other teachers in their buildings and districts (Wood & Lieberman, 2000).

COMPOSING WRITING, COMPOSING TEACHING

Writing in the Writing Project has given me permission to trust my own thinking. It's given me connections to resources—both human and otherwise—to nurture my development and the development of others. It's given me time to think about what I think. (TC, Interview, 1999)

Because part of the NWP's original and ongoing mission is to develop good teachers of writing, the summer institutes place a strong emphasis on writing. Writing, NWP teachers tell us, is a powerful form of learning. It gives articulate form to internal mental processes and, in one teacher consultant's words, provides a "pathway to learning" (Interview, 1998). Writing produces occasions to foreground and clarify thinking; to record, shape, and analyze experiences; to express internal lives; to explore ideas learned from others. Writers have opportunities to discern both what they understand and what they have yet to learn (Atwell, 1987; Atwell-Vasey, 1998; Calkins, 1994; Graves, 1983). The NWP approach is to teach writing as a *social* process, that is, not only as a medium for self-expression but also as a vehicle for learning-in-community. Writing within a highly participatory community gives people the chance to learn about themselves, one another, and the world. Furthermore, it provides writers an authentic audience with whom to assess and improve their efforts.

The writing-workshop model might be, in fact, a loose metaphor to describe the professional development that occurs in the NWP network. In a writing workshop, the process of writing unfolds in public. It both requires and creates community as people share their writing and respond to the writing of others in the group. Writers work through recursive, nonlinear composing processes that involve planning, intending, choosing, drafting, sharing, revising, and publishing. These composing processes are not steps toward a predetermined goal. They unfold organically, sometimes backtrack, and sometimes leap ahead.

Fundamental to the workshop model is an underlying assumption that deep understanding arises from *practice*. Thus, writers are the best teachers of writers simply because they are involved in the practice of writing. For the same reason, teachers are the best teachers of teachers. By taking the position that those who *practice* writing or teaching are most likely to be good at *teaching* it, the NWP privileges both an expertise rooted in practice and a non-hierarchical, peer-to-peer approach to teaching and learning. An experienced TC made these connections clearly:

> Well, I think number one is that if I'm a teacher of writing I have to be a writer. That's, I guess, the biggest idea. If I'm going to be a teacher of reading, I have to be a reader. I have to continue to grow as a reader; I can't just stop and only read the things I read when I was in school and only read the things that my students are going to read. Then, the next step I learned was I need to share my teaching with other teachers. And now I know I have some good ideas that other people would like to hear about. (Interview, 1999)

With remarkable congruency, the NWP has developed an approach to professional development that echoes the recursive processes of composing writing. Just as prewriting begins with the intentions and ideas of writers, NWP professional development begins with practitioners and builds on their prior knowledge, experience, and commitments. With regard to drafting, the NWP encourages teachers, like writers, to think about their practices as simply the latest best effort. Conceived in this way, teaching practices are always open to critique, refinement, and improvement. Peer review provides necessary feedback for revision and encourages teachers to "come clean" with their struggles and challenges and to remain open to critique. When teachers "publish"—that is, make their practices public, whether inside or outside the NWP—

they join in a collective enterprise to build and disseminate practitioner knowledge. The intense writing that goes on in the summer institutes and beyond encourages and amplifies teachers' voices, releases their knowledge and perspectives, surfaces their questions and problems, and creates communities of mutual concern and helpful critique. In this way, these processes establish essential grounds for professional learning communities.

SOCIAL PRACTICES LEADING TO PROFESSIONAL COMMUNITY

It's invigorating for me to see teachers inventing and creating themselves and not waiting for someone outside to do it for them. There's just such a difference between teachers who are really letting the creative juices flow and teachers who are just turning the pages. There's a difference for the kids. (Principal, Focus Group, 1999)

What is key here is that going through these stages of writing as a community mirrors the social practices that saturate interactions and activities within the NWP community, whether or not they are directly related to writing. Wenger (1998) has written about "learning as social participation," making the claim that participation in communities of practitioners "shapes not only what we do, but also who we are and how we interpret what we do" (p. 4). For him, such communities become arenas for professional learning because the people in them imbue activities with shared meanings, develop a sense of belonging, and create new identities based, in part, on their relationships with one another.

This is precisely what we saw happening in NWP learning communities. The social practices adopted by the NWP convey norms and purposes, they create a sense of belonging, and they shape professional identities. The teachers we saw enacting the social practices of the NWP surrendered reliance on routine and conventional teaching approaches in order to continuously search for better ways to meet students' needs, and they saw themselves as conducting this search not only as individuals but also as members of a professional community.

Our research revealed that the NWP engages in the following social practices:

- Approaching each colleague as a potentially valuable contributor
- Honoring teacher knowledge
- Creating public forums for teacher sharing, dialogue, and critique
- Turning ownership of learning over to learners
- Situating human learning in practice and relationships
- Providing multiple entry points into the learning community
- Guiding reflection on teaching through reflection on learning
- Sharing leadership
- Promoting a stance of inquiry
- Encouraging a reconceptualization of professional identity and linking it to professional community

It is important to emphasize that these practices are interactive and mutually dependent and that together they have the power to generate teaching cultures very unlike those of typical schools. Isolating the practices for purposes of analysis, as we do below, unfortunately misrepresents how they work in reality. In fact, we suspect that it is only in a culture that works consciously and persistently to integrate them that they can truly reinforce and sustain one another.

Approaching Each Colleague as a Potentially Valuable Contributor

It is one thing to speak of a participatory community rhetorically and quite another to create a community in which every member actually *does* participate. As good writing teachers try to draw on the authentic voices and experiences of potential writers, the NWP approaches every teacher as if what he or she thinks and has experienced matters. A site director explained, "it was intended in the Writing Project community that in the summer institute . . . there be an unconditional acceptance of who they [teachers] are, what they believe, and what they think" (Interview, 1998). Treating teachers this way makes them more willing to take the risk of contributing and belonging to a professional community. It provides a powerful antidote to the isolation and silence all too typical of many teachers' professional lives (Cohn & Kottkamp, 1993; Goodlad, 1984; Lieberman & Miller, 1999; Little, 1999; Lortie, 1975).

It is essential, as Greene (1978, 1995) reminds us, to treat all learners not as mere receptacles for others' ideas but as if they are engaged in their own quests and projects, as if, in other words, they are purposeful protagonists in their own lives. One teacher described the breakthrough she experienced when she was approached in this way: "The big thing for me was recognizing I do know something and that others can benefit when I share it" (TC, Interview, 1998). A site director talked about how valuable it is to be open to colleagues:

> We need what other people know. And this could be the person sitting next to us in the summer institute, or the teacher down the hall. . . . It's about starting with where everyone is and what they know about teaching and their field and acknowledging that to learn, we need to find our own answers together. And part of that is simply by listening. (Interview, 1999)

In brief, this social practice invites every member of the community to develop and raise his or her voice so that he or she has the potential to make a unique contribution. Perhaps more subtly, it serves as an impetus for ongoing learning. When teachers are expected to contribute, they want to make certain they are continually developing something *worthy* to contribute.

Honoring Teacher Knowledge

Fundamental to the NWP approach to professional development is the practice of teachers teaching other teachers. NWP teachers teach colleagues in workshops, conferences, professional conversations, writing groups, teaching demonstrations, and so forth. This comprehensive practice topples traditional hierarchies, which presume that knowledge resides in the authority of recognized experts or accepted theory (Grumet, 1988; Minnich, 1990; Schön, 1983). In the process, it releases what teachers have learned from practice. One site director explained:

> We always start with what teachers know. The Writing Project is really an invitation for teachers to share what they know. . . .The research in the Writing Project is about teachers' questions and the assumption is that teachers *have* questions and that they are thinking about their practice. We try to share what we know and we have a support system right alongside us, and they—our colleagues—provide what they know. (Interview, 1998)

To adopt this social practice, then, requires a dual commitment from teachers. They must share what they know and take seriously what others know, the assumption being that everyone has something both to teach and to learn. Most experience greater self-confidence as learners because they know they have capable peers on whom they can depend for advice and guidance. Moreover, when teachers teach other teachers, they surface collective knowledge and expertise. Those participating take pride not only in their own accomplishments but also in their profession. Professional learning becomes not merely a solitary enterprise but also a group responsibility.

Creating Public Forums for Teacher Sharing, Dialogue, and Critique

Key to breaking through teacher isolation and silence are the public forums that the NWP creates for teachers to share their work and then critique and discuss it. Throughout the summer institute, as we have described, teachers take center stage to read their writing or demonstrate a teaching practice. What is more, they come to expect other teachers to do the same. We saw veteran TCs creating multiple ways to take their work public, such as presentations for parents and professional conferences, articles for professional journals, conversations via electronic conferencing, or contributions to local newsletters and newspapers.

Crucial to what NWP teachers learn from going public with their work is the role of critical dialogue. In preparation for playing a more public role, institute fellows learn to give and take criticism in a professional fashion. They develop a common investment in the quality of their public contributions. Despite the potential for interpersonal difficulties, most NWP teachers refuse to lapse into a comfortable "niceness" that obstructs opportunities to grow. They realize that if people are to learn from public performances, then collegial criticism is essential. Public presentation, critique, reflection, and self-critique become community norms.

More recently, making practitioner knowledge public has moved into the political arena. NWP teachers are increasingly engaged in lobbying legislators on the state and national levels, influencing district officials, and presenting to local school boards and parents. This active participation in civic life and educational policy arenas is all too rare among K–12 teachers. But the NWP has demonstrated that such participation brings a valuable and sorely needed perspective to the ongoing public conversations about education.

Turning Ownership of Learning over to Learners

Wherever we went, we heard NWP teachers talking about the importance of turning learning over to students so that they would develop a sense of ownership for it. Without that sense of ownership, they argued, learners are rarely truly engaged or motivated. In this spirit, the NWP insists on professional development opportunities that are solidly teacher-centered. Teachers name their own problems and articulate important issues and then have the autonomy to design learning experiences around these.

A TC in a focus group summed it up this way, "The thing is to give total responsibility to the students for their own learning, and then take responsibility for my own learning. That sort of says it all"(Focus Group, 1999). Just as they turn ownership of learning

over to their students, they take ownership of their own professional development, which results in an enhanced sense of professional responsibility. This turns the current, prevalent idea about
teacher accountability, as assessed through standardized tests, on
its head. NWP teachers practice accountability as measured by
how they see students responding in their classrooms. They feel
responsible for engaging their students and seeking out ways to
make learning relevant to their lives. They are accountable not in
response to outside monitoring, but rather because they are continually assessing students' progress and gauging their practice
accordingly. Moreover, they belong to a professional community
that demonstrates repeatedly how professional learning and student learning are mutually dependent and intertwined.

Situating Human Learning in Practice and Relationships

Teachers in the NWP learn from practice—the practice of writing and the practice of teaching. Through their experiences in the
institutes and beyond, they see that meaningful learning is both
active and relational. Learning-by-doing and learning-in-relation-
ships become for them essential principles guiding classroom
teaching and their own professional development. We were struck
with how many TCs told us they surrendered "teaching-as-
telling" after the summer institute and replaced it with efforts to
build authentic learning communities. One TC said:

> I build a community in my classroom every year, which is
> one of those things that was most valuable to me as a learn-
> er in the summer institute. You experience for yourself
> what's valuable to help you be a writer and learner there,
> and you want your students to have the same experience.
> (Focus Group, 1999)

Creating the kind of community that nourishes learning is, of
course, complicated work, whether in the classroom or in a professional development initiative. When people learn not just by
listening but by actively undertaking some project or task, they
must take risks. They need communities where interpersonal

relationships are a priority, so that tolerance and compassion are extended when mistakes are made. As a TC explained, "When we have doubts, we know that we can turn to someone with the same set of values" (Interview, 1999). Teachers who want to learn in a professional community need to be able to depend on constructive critique and helpful suggestions from their peers. NWP teachers learn, therefore, to place a high priority on learners' relationships, both with one another and among students in their classrooms—not in the name of "feel-good" interactions, but to establish a vigorous intellectual context for learning (Wood & Lieberman, 2000).

Providing Multiple Entry Points in to the Learning Community

We were struck with how many ways teachers described the benefits of belonging to the NWP community. We met teachers who came to the network because they were searching for new strategies to motivate students to read and write. We met teachers hungry for lesson plans and teaching resources. Some teachers came because they wanted to share their talents and expertise with other teachers. Others wanted the opportunity to explore their own writing. Some expressed a need for a professional community. Still others simply felt honored by the invitation and came into the community not knowing what to expect.

By providing multiple entry points for engagement to meet all these needs, the NWP avoids an ideological perspective and, in fact, succeeds in promoting a kind of pluralism. Teachers come into the fold with many different perspectives, interests, and concerns. The NWP offers "no great truth" (Site Director, Interview, 1998), but rather offers an opportunity for teachers to come together to name and investigate their own challenges and problems. NWP teachers tend to have little faith in ready-made solutions purported to work under any circumstances with any student. Most NWP teachers, in fact, learn to "embrace contraries" (Elbow, 1986) or to create new syntheses out of apparent dualities. They recognize that being a good teacher requires exploration of both technique and philosophy, both personal responsibility and community involvement, a concern for both individuals and the good of the community, both knowledge from the inside and knowledge from without. The needs of individual learners demand a repertoire of responses, not adherence to a strict ideology. Because teachers come to the NWP for a wide variety of reasons, they bring a diversity of perspectives, interests, and talents that are constantly revitalizing and enriching the growing community.

Guiding Reflection on Teaching Through Reflection on Learning

Unfortunately, much professional development is based on a simplistic, linear conception of the relationship between teaching and learning (Smith, 1995; Wenger, 1998), or, in other words, on the notion that teaching *causes* learning. Consequently, typical in-services frequently promote "best practices" ostensibly designed to promote learning for all students. The NWP, on the other hand, begins with a focus on learning. The powerful learning that institute fellows experience during their 5-week initiation begins that journey. NWP teachers told us repeatedly that, by thinking and talking about what happened to them during the institutes, they came to see that they learned not because they were "taught" per se, but because they had the space and time to articulate, research, discuss, and write about what they wanted to know—all within the context of a learning community. It was their experiences and interactions with other professional teachers, combined with the reflection and self-expression involved in writing, that made learning meaningful and powerful.

In line with the idea that the best teachers of any practice are practitioners themselves, the NWP promotes the notion that the best teachers for learners are themselves learners. We repeatedly found that NWP teachers come away from the institute vowing to change their teaching, not simply because they have learned new ideas and strategies from one another but also because they have learned from their own experiences as learners. This happens by design.

Frequently during the institute, facilitators will hold a "status-of-the-class" session, asking participants to think about how and what they are learning and what they would like to change about the proceedings. By having repeated opportunities to reflect on what, for most fellows, tend to be powerful learning experiences, and then thinking about the conditions that foster them, NWP teachers gain insights into the learning process itself. They pay heightened attention to the frustrations, fears, joys, and triumphs of being a learner. It is, of course, currently fashionable to recommend reflection on practice. But what seems especially valuable about the NWP approach is that reflection begins with *learning* and then moves out to teaching.

Sharing Leadership

One of the most obvious practices of the NWP community is the sharing of leadership. Starting with the summer institute—when each individual fellow takes a turn at the author's chair, demonstrates a lesson, logs activities, and so forth—the culture sets a norm for rotating leadership responsibilities. Fellows become accustomed to and practiced in playing leadership roles and then encounter a myriad of opportunities to continue their leadership roles—both formally and informally—after the institute. Once having recognized their potential for leadership, many NWP teachers practice it enthusiastically in a variety of ways. Some become leaders in their own buildings. Some contribute to the professional development of colleagues in their schools and beyond. Some even become involved politically, working to ensure policies friendly to "the work."

A TC described for us some of the roles she has taken on over the years:

> I usually lead a group or two of teachers during the year. Last year I had a teacher research group and the Focus on Standards group. The FOS *group* traveled a lot because we had to meet with TCs from other California Writing Project sites. I am also on the advisory committee. . . . I also feel a need to be a voice for urban teachers. This is one of the reasons I am part of the leadership team. As we make plans, I think about what will be helpful to teachers in schools like mine and the schools my children attend. (Interview, 2000)

Promoting a Stance of Inquiry

Permeating the entire NWP culture is the idea that constant questioning and searching are fundamental to good teaching. A veteran TC told us that the NWP helped her

> gain this kind of inquiring stance into what I do, and to keep looking for answers when things aren't going in a right direction, to try to look at some evidence or data to try to figure it out. What could make it work better, or why isn't it working right, or, well, what else should I be doing here? (Interview, 1999)

Such a stance frequently leads TCs to teacher research. Perhaps this attitude also accounts for the uncanny capacity of NWP teachers to stay positive. Repeatedly, we heard TCs praising their own community for not becoming mired in habits of complaining. As one site director put it:

> This kind of professional development invites teachers, me included, to share our best stories as opposed to the day-to-day talk in the faculty lounge. More negative talk happens there. In a Writing Project event, there's no time for the negative. But that isn't to say we don't look at the hard issues. It's just that we don't dwell in the negative. There's no time. There's too much to do. (Interview, 1999)

This propensity to be positive, rooted solidly in a strong sense of responsibility to students, demonstrates the faith NWP teachers hold that together they can find better ways to reach students. The focus rests very little on "what works." Instead, it scans the horizon for how to improve.

Encouraging a Reconceptualization of Professional Identity and Linking It to Professional Community

A TC told us that she thought of "writing as a bridge" that enables learners to make connections with content, their teachers, and their colleagues (Interview, 1998). We saw the truth of her statement during the summer institutes when we witnessed how writing provides a bridge between individual fellows and the larger community. The self-disclosure necessarily involved in the sharing of writing creates a web of connections and draws the community closer. Because collaboration is so central to their experiences in the summer institutes, most NWP teachers quite consciously internalize the value of professional community over time. They recognize that as they invest in and learn from colleagues, their work with students becomes richer, more rewarding, and even easier.

Thus, NWP teachers tend to develop professional identities, which demand high levels of collaboration. We were struck repeatedly with how frequently they use "we" instead of "I." Ownership of exciting ideas and strategies is *collective* ownership, and professional knowledge is held by the community as well as by individuals. Similarly, professional responsibility for students' learning is no longer the responsibility of a teacher working alone in his or her classroom; it becomes a responsibility of the professional community. To be a Writing Project teacher is to be a colleague.

A case in point occurred when we somewhat reluctantly approached a TC to help us with our research project, knowing that she was terribly busy. When we asked if she was certain she could take on this extra task, she commented, "Oh, I always know that I'm going to get more out of it than I put in whenever I get involved in something like this. Anything involved with the Writing Project is always like that." TCs perceive participation in the NWP community as generating more energy than it drains. For TCs, quality teaching becomes a matter of staying intellectually vital and curious, and participating in a professional community is a good way of going about that.

THE "WORK": SETTING CULTURAL CONDITIONS FOR PROFESSIONAL LEARNING

The "work" of the NWP is fundamentally about learning what it means to be a learner and understanding in important ways what it means to help others learn. In NWP terms, however, both can only be accomplished by establishing a set of social practices that transform how people think of themselves and how they interact with colleagues in a learning community. Because these practices are founded on principles of inclusion and pluralism, they tend to create learning communities capable of avoiding the ideological conflicts with the potential to tear communities apart (Westheimer, 1998).

Currently, there is a great deal of public talk about teacher accountability, usually defined in terms of students' test scores. TCs believe, however, that the NWP fosters a kind of teacher accountability much more likely to ensure students' academic success. Professional accountability, on their terms, means (1) expecting every child to learn and (2) sharing one's expertise and seeking the counsel of others. A seasoned TC explained that participation in a professional community "keeps us caring and enthusiastic over the years" (Interview, 1998). Another told us that, "the Writing Project is an angel on my shoulder"(Interview, 1999).

The alchemy of the NWP, then, is really the enactment of social practices capable of building relationships, stimulating learning, developing voice and efficacy, and conveying professional purpose. No one could say it better than this TC, describing what the "work" had done for her:

> It's changed my life outside my teaching, inside my teaching. It's literally changed my whole life. It's given me a support system; it's given me friends; it's given me my writing back; it's given me my classroom back. (Focus Group, 1999)

Having seen how these practices seemed to build communities and transform individuals, we wanted to understand how the NWP spreads its influence, while sustaining its integrity and effectiveness. We turned to look carefully at the organization of the NWP as a network.

Chapter 3

Growing the Network

People get the idea that this is an invitation. This is a place
where you can bring yourself and what you know. And there's
a community of people that would support you at a variety of
levels. . . . It's a safe place to try out an idea and then some-
times you find people that want to help you with it.

(Site Director, Interview, 1998)

What keeps me invested is that when I hear something at a
conference, workshop, meeting, or casual conversation that is
working for someone else, it energizes me and makes me
want to try it or, in some ways, to improve what I am doing.
Being in the WP is a continual renewal for me.

(Teacher Consultant, Interview, 2000)

The way we work is deeply influenced by the local level.
Going to the summer institute, being a teacher consultant and
then a director helped shape me. I scout talent. I make con-
nections between and among organizations, inspire vision, lis-
ten to people. I put language to it.

(Elyse Aidman-Aadahl, Interview, 2000)

We have seen that the idea of "the work" of the NWP encompasses a set of social practices—practices that involve new people
as participants in the community, providing them with the means
to learn from as well as to make contributions to it. Many teachers begin to see themselves and their work differently as they
experience putting their practice at the center, recognizing that
what they know and produce as writers is the starting point for
their involvement, understanding, and eventual improvement

(St. John et al., 2001). Writing and learning are joined in such powerful ways that teachers speak about how they are "transformed," "jazzed," "exhilarated."

While there are a number of professional development efforts where teachers get excited about a good workshop and feel that they have learned a great deal, what makes the NWP unique is that at the summer institutes the seeds of a network are sown and nurtured. Teachers commit themselves not only to the many strategies, lessons, and approaches that they encounter during the summer institutes but also to the ideals and goals that are larger than their classroom, school, or district, unbounded by geographic location or role or level of schooling. The central social practice of linking professional identity to professional community enables the NWP to transcend the limitations of traditional workshops given on professional development days. Indeed, every NWP summer institute creates a new culture in which teachers' knowledge is central rather than peripheral, and critiqued and nuanced rather than hidden—a culture where carrying inquiry into practice becomes the norm. The social practices that arise from the activities teachers participate in are not just a one-time thing; they are incorporated into the lives of those who participate in the NWP community. As we saw with the teachers we followed, both the new and the experienced teachers brought these practices into their classrooms and their schools.

To understand the full impact of the NWP, it is necessary to look at it from an *organizational* perspective, since its network-like qualities—with flexible, borderless, adaptive structures—support scores of local sites while maintaining a strong national presence. When we looked for the connection between the social practices that we saw in the activities that took place during the summer and the network-like organizational structure that seemed to both spread and deepen the work, we were told repeatedly that "if you want to understand the NWP, you can see it all in the summer institute." So we began there, looking at what NWP participants do at the institute as well as what transpires after it is over.

THE SUMMER INSTITUTE AS
THE CENTRAL ORGANIZING UNIT

From the beginning we observed that there was something about the commitment of effort, time, and resources that signaled to teachers that the summer institute was no ordinary professional development workshop. Many teachers had also heard about it from their friends, since NWP teachers encourage their peers to attend so that they can share the experience with them. We were beginning to get a sense of why the summer institute was so critical to understanding the NWP and why it might give us a clue as to how and why the local networks function.

The invitational accepts 18 to 22 experienced teachers from K–16 and from all disciplines. Those who are accepted are given a small stipend for their attendance and are expected to bring a teaching practice with them that they will demonstrate for their peers. The experience is so powerful that, within 5 weeks, strangers from different kinds of schools, and often without shared backgrounds or beliefs, come together and, as a group, share their practices with one another, write and present something themselves, critique one another's work, give constructive feedback to their peers on their writing, read and discuss research and contemporary literature, and become part of a community of fellow teachers who accept improving one's practice as a norm for being a teacher.

Teachers find that in making their strategies public they become more aware of their intentions, their knowledge of their subject matter, and the influence of context on their students and themselves. When their peers give them feedback, they experience what it means to go public and to talk with other adults who care about the same things they do. This helps to clarify their awareness of what they know and what they need to learn.

As the summer goes on, leadership opportunities arise. Some teachers find it rewarding to teach adults, to share their teaching dilemmas and engage them in efforts to find alternative solutions. During the institute, the site directors look for teachers who have developed effective teaching strategies that they have honed and nuanced over the years, and who show by their participation in the institute that they are internalizing the NWP perspective on professional development. Although everyone is theoretically a *teacher consultant,* or TC, when the institute is over, some become active in teaching other teachers and discover the power of teaching adults, while others stay connected through the yearly conferences or other leadership activities run by their local network. One teacher consultant put it like this:

> On one level TCs work a lot on their own teaching. The continued discussions with teachers about teaching, whether giving a presentation or at meetings regarding new WP projects, you deepen your understanding of practice and theory. On another level, you learn a lot about teacher learning through experience. It is not explicit . . . you have to stretch your thinking as a presenter as to what texts and structures you can use to give your audience a chance to experience the presentation rather than watch it. (Interview, 2000)

In a recent study of the NWP, it was found that most teachers who took part in the study took on leadership roles in their school, district, or state (Fancsali & Nelsestuen, 2001).

To build on the work of the summer institute, teachers are encouraged to come to a variety of activities that are organized throughout the year as participants or as teacher consultants. Some teachers are so enthusiastic that they try to re-create their summer experiences, adapting the social practices of the summer institute to their own schools and contexts. As a second-grade teacher stated:

> I did in-service for my school right after I took the summer institute. We did snacks, wrote poetry. People came up with amazing stuff. We worked in groups and charted everything. They agreed that we have to start a writing group. (Interview, 1998)

TEACHER CONSULTANTS:
DEVELOPING THE LEADERSHIP OF THE NETWORK

Becoming a teacher consultant is recognized as both an opportunity for growth and as a way to make a professional contribution to teaching as well as to the NWP. Teachers are paid for providing workshops, becoming coaches, leading special-interest groups, and more. What is fundamental to the work of the summer institute is the idea that teachers need opportunities to grow and change, to share their practices with others, and to expand their horizons beyond the classroom. Teachers are encouraged to stay connected, to continue to shape the network, and to take responsibility for leadership of the network. Some become leaders of a new kind of professional development in their school or district and, as new initiatives arise, take the lead in organizing and/or running them. They become the backbone of the network, leading a variety of professional development initiatives while increasing their own opportunities to learn.

The summer institute is the first iteration of "the model," which encompasses the social practices of the NWP. As some members of each new group of NWP participants become TCs, new communities arise within which new identities are shaped, new roles are created, and new opportunities beyond the institute become available. For each participant who becomes a teacher consultant, 15 other teachers are being served by the NWP. This ratio has remained constant over the last 5 years (St. John, 1999). In other words, as teachers learn to teach other teachers they provide professional development for these teachers or lead study groups or special-interest groups for their site. While the process varies at different sites, the figures indicate the continued growth of the NWP as a network, as it involves new teachers and, at the same time, develops a strong leadership cadre from among its teacher participants. Observing both the UCLA and OSU sites in depth, we began to understand both the similarities and differences of each site as they responded to their local settings, as well as the ways in which program activities are adapted to the particularities of state and local contexts.

THE UCLA WRITING PROJECT: AN URBAN SITE

The UCLA Writing Project (UCLA WP) is situated in Los Angeles, which has the second-largest school district in the country. Its public school population of 800,000 has become increasingly multiethnic: about 65% Latino, 14.4% African American, 12.1% White, 5% Asian, .3% Native American, and 1.9% Pacific Islander. Proposition 227, which limits a student to 1 year of bilingual classes without a special waiver, and high-stakes testing, with standardized tests being used as the criteria for passing and failing courses and graduating from high school, are two recent developments that greatly affect the process of teaching and learning in the district.

The UCLA Writing Project has a university director, a co-director and three associate directors (all working teachers), and an advisory board that meets four times a year to make decisions about the summer program and any new initiatives it chooses to start. The 25-year-old site was one of the first eight sites in California, funded by a grant to the National Writing Project from the National Endowment for the Humanities. Subsequently, the UCLA Writing Project followed, along with 17 other sites in California, also affiliated with the California Subject Matter Projects, created by the state of California after 1987 to improve instruction in a variety of disciplines. Thus, the UCLA Writing Project enjoys associations in three interwoven networks: the California Writing Project, the California Subject Matter Projects, and the National Writing Project.

During its 25-year history at UCLA, the project has had offices in a variety of locations on and off campus. Only within the last 5 years has it been housed within the School of Education on the UCLA campus. In 1995 the UCLA WP became a part of Center X, created by Jeannie Oakes, a professor at UCLA in the school of education. The purpose of Center X is to provide a place and a forum where theory and practice meet, and that involves teachers, schools, and the university in the development of innovative practices. Housing the UCLA WP within Center X was an important signal of an approach toward teaching practice in the school of education and the importance of the Writing Project to its educational programs. Both implicitly and explicitly, the center recognized that knowledge was being created by teachers in the schools as well as by teachers in the university. While the writing project was incorporated into the pre-service teacher education program within a few years, it also maintained its independence as a site for teacher in-service. In essence, part of its work has become integrated into the university, as another part remains independent of the school of education. This unique arrangement has allowed the WP to work with beginning teachers, as it continues to expand and deepen its work with experienced teachers in the field. As Figure 3.1 shows, the UCLA WP has made adaptations to the changing policy context of California, while maintaining a cultural context of its own. It is important to note that this figure was made to represent the policy context in 1999. The context does not stay the same, nor should it be seen as representative of what the context is today. In fact its continuous adaptation to changes in district and state policy, without losing the essentials of the NWP, has kept it viable and growing.

The UCLA WP is part of national, state, and local contexts. As explained in Chapter 1, the Bay Area Writing Project, the first site, was organized in 1973–1974 by James Gray, a senior lecturer at the University of California at Berkeley. The national headquarters of the writing project is still housed there. The California Writing Project (CWP), made up of 18 different sites in the state, meets two times a year, giving the local sites a chance to discuss and work together on ways of dealing with the often shifting California policy context of which they are all a part. In addition, representatives of all sites attend the yearly meeting of the National Council of Teachers of English (NCTE), where the Writing Project holds its annual meeting. The network connections are broad, since UCLA teachers can connect to other sites in the state, to the national office, and to people from all over the country at the national meeting. (Some even consult with other Writing Project sites in other parts of the country when their particular expertise is needed.)

The structure of the UCLA WP has been flexible enough to allow it to grow and develop while it continues to adapt its work to changing contextual conditions. For example, several summer offerings reflect the changing policy context for teachers in

Figure 3.1
UCLA Writing Project

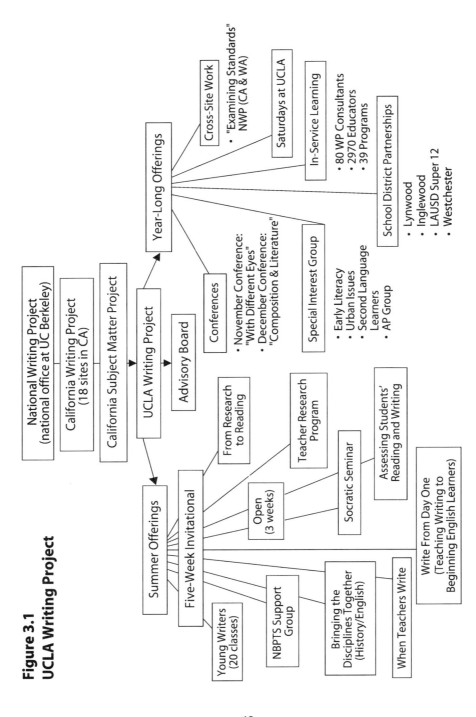

National Writing Project
(national office at UC Berkeley)

California Writing Project
(18 sites in CA)

California Subject Matter Project

UCLA Writing Project

Advisory Board

Summer Offerings

Year-Long Offerings

Five-Week Invitational

From Research to Reading

Open (3 weeks)

Teacher Research Program

Socratic Seminar

Assessing Students' Reading and Writing

Young Writers (20 classes)

NBPTS Support Group

Bringing the Disciplines Together (History/English)

When Teachers Write

Write From Day One (Teaching Writing to Beginning English Learners)

Conferences
- November Conference: "With Different Eyes"
- December Conference: "Composition & Literature"

Special Interest Group
- Early Literacy
- Urban Issues
- Second Language Learners
- AP Group

Cross-Site Work
- "Examining Standards" NWP (CA & WA)

Saturdays at UCLA

In-Service Learning
- 80 WP Consultants
- 2970 Educators
- 39 Programs

School District Partnerships
- Lynwood
- Inglewood
- LAUSD Super 12
- Westchester

California. The National Board for Professional Teaching
Standards (NBPTS) has offered a substantial bonus to teachers
who pass the National Board. The UCLA WP has responded by
creating a support group for teachers (led by a teacher consultant),
which begins in the summer and meets throughout the year to
help teachers pass the Board. From Research to Reading, an initiative from the Governor's office, is another teacher development
issue taken on by the UCLA WP. Because of its expertise and experience with problems of literacy, the Writing Project volunteered to
sponsor part of the program under its auspices. In this way the
Writing Project is connected to, yet maintains its independence
from, statewide initiatives. The "Open" is a 3-week professional
development opportunity based on the 5-week invitational, but
open to anyone who applies. "Write From Day One" was developed as a summer workshop that helps teachers develop skills
and abilities with second-language learners.

Throughout the year the site provides a range of activities for
participants to stay connected to the Writing Project community.
Because this is an older site, there are already four different school
or district partnerships that have been developed by the Writing
Project. Led by people in the field, or sometimes by the Writing
Project itself, they involve working with a district, a set of schools,
or different groups of teachers. All of these different types of
arrangements provide professional development with TCs as their
leaders. More sporadic, but no less important, are 1-day workshops
on Saturdays throughout the year where teachers come together to
share their work and their dilemmas, learn new strategies, and connect once again to their newfound community. In addition, Writing
Project co-directors take requests from around the city for in-service work. The number of teacher consultants and the number of
programs that they are involved in testify to the importance of this
NWP site to the Los Angeles educational community.

Special-interest groups whose objectives reflect the needs of the
urban population served by this site are encouraged. Led by
teacher consultants, the groups focus on early literacy among
young students, urban issues affecting adolescents, and working
with second-language learners. A new initiative, a special-interest
group on Advanced Placement, is studying how and in what ways

the UCLA WP can become involved in the preparation for high school Advanced Placement courses.

Figure 3.1 of the UCLA WP site indicates the organizational and programmatic connections: the context, the governing structure, and the summer and yearly offerings. The advisory board discusses potential programs and how they can be initiated and supported. For example, when Inglewood Schools were sued for not providing AP classes in their schools (thus putting their students at a disadvantage in getting into the University of California), the UCLA WP realized that this was an urban issue as well as an Inglewood issue and decided to start the special-interest group that year to discuss how they might participate. When the national office created a project to examine standards, it invited UCLA WP and other writing project sites in California and Washington to be project partners, since they both had mandated standards. (Six sites in these two states worked together on a common issue, tied together by their membership in the NWP). Seminars, workshops, conferences, special-interest groups, partnerships, in-services, and so on are all forms that are used to engage teachers in dealing with a variety of issues that focus on teaching in an urban setting.

The 5-week invitational and the "Open" program remain constant, since they are the core offerings of the WP. Some summer initiatives, such as providing for classes for young writers (given in schools) continue to grow; some new offerings may be created while others are phased out. This is a major advantage of network organization: It can shape the network and its activities to the needs of its members and the social context of its community. The ability of this national network to create new sites, while supporting its existing ones, enables it to continue to increase its significance to educational reform. It is an effective example of "scaling down" (providing a model that can be organized locally) while continuing to "scale up" (spreading the model throughout the nation) (McDonald, 1996, p. 247). While the social practices provide a universal way of working, local sites make particularistic adaptations that help them root the strategy in local soil. Looking at the Oklahoma State University Writing Project (OSU WP) next, we can see both the universal practices that have become normative in the NWP and the particular adaptations made in this case of a site that includes rural, suburban, and urban communities.

THE OKLAHOMA STATE UNIVERSITY WRITING PROJECT: A REGIONAL SITE

Our second site is 8 years old and housed at Oklahoma State University in Stillwater, Oklahoma. The current site leader has been at the site since 1993, when she was a co-director, giving the site important continuity of leadership. An English professor at the university is a co-director. At OSU, a Writing Council serves as an advisory group. Its members include about 15 TCs, who receive a small stipend for their time, and representatives from different program areas such as the Youth Writing Project, Teacher Research, or newsletter editor. Some teachers choose to serve because they are interested in the work and want to participate in some way. The council, which meets three or four times a year, cannot make the day-to-day decisions for the OSU WP, but it does make policy decisions that give direction and overall vision. It is also used as a way to cultivate leadership, disseminate information, and build the capacity of the site (Director's Interview, 2001).

The service area, covering the northern half of Oklahoma, incorporates a range of locations from tiny towns and farm communities to affluent suburbs and impoverished urban areas. The predominately rural area makes it difficult to build up a critical mass of TCs (a strategy carried out in the UCLA WP). Instead, the director and the TCs work to create a wide variety of offerings that try to overcome the limitations of distance and sparse population. Rather than being defeated by the distances, the site makes special efforts to reach out and work with existing programs, piggy-back on other meetings to make best use of time and travel, and offer a variety of professional development activities suited to the time and place where they are held. The director, TCs, and teachers must drive long distances to get to WP events. Meetings must be planned to start late and end early to accommodate to these conditions, and budgeting for activities must often include lodging. In this setting new technology has played a crucial role in communicating and connecting people with one another.

The State Department of Education has initiated a series of reforms over the past 10 years, changing policies so often that teachers rarely have enough time to incorporate them before new demands are made, leaving the teachers demoralized rather than enthusiastic about their work. Within this context the OSU WP site has, by involving teachers in quality professional development activities, grown and expanded its influence.

During the past 3 years the OSU WP was one of the sites chosen for Project Outreach, an effort on behalf of the National Writing Project to increase the sites' connection to underserved schools and teachers. The OSU WP has also been a member of the NWP Rural Sites Network, which has helped bring additional resources to this area, particularly technology. Both the funding from Project Outreach (organized by the National Writing Project and externally funded) and the Rural Sites Network (federally funded) have involved this site in developing ways to combat rural isolation.

One way to deal with increasing the variety of offerings, yet provide a measure of consistency, has been to create a "model" that can be transported to any school in the geographical area. The model at the OSU WP consists of teacher demonstrations, teacher writing and writing groups, as well as research facilitated by TCs that teachers do in their own classrooms. This model has been used for mentoring new teachers and also for encouraging more experienced teachers to improve the teaching of writing and literacy. The model contains the essential practices of the NWP: Involve teachers in doing their own writing, have teachers teach each other, and build a community that respects and honors teacher knowledge *as the starting point* for growth and development. Figure 3.2 helps show how the model takes root, and how it spreads and deepens. This diagram presents the activities of the OSU site in 1999. Because of the strength and character of this site, the diagram will change over time. Some activities will grow, some will most likely be dropped, and others will be organized. As pointed out earlier, it is the power of these local site networks that they stay close to their participants, while recognizing the particularities of their policy contexts.

Figure 3.2
Oklahoma State
University Writing Project

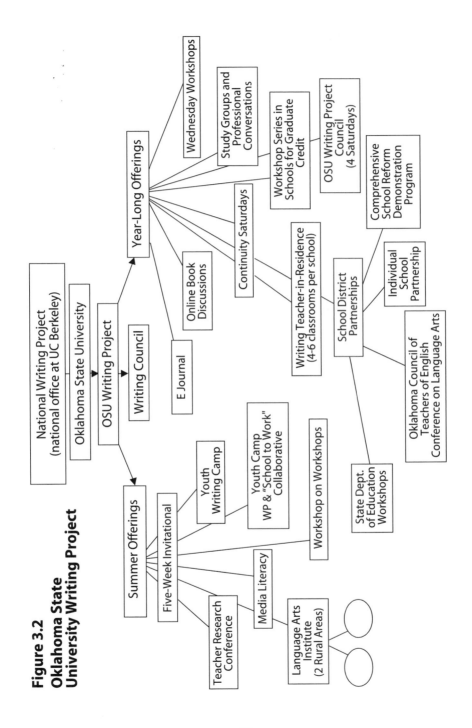

As in other NWP sites, there is a 5-week invitational institute held during the summer. At this invitational, teachers learn to do research, and some of them attend a Teacher Research Conference, where further opportunities are provided for TCs to share their research with an ever-expanding teacher group.

Other activities during the summer include two Language Arts Institutes, given in cooperation with the State Department of Education at more remote rural locations (TCs work in teams planning day and evening workshops and events), and a student writing camp whose theme is connecting school to work. Students learn about the world of work through a variety of activities. In these as in other projects, the OSU WP makes connections with other organizations helping to interpret and develop state policy initiatives. Following the summer institute, there is a "workshop on workshops." TCs learn about workshop design and presentation techniques that help them to understand and practice what they have experienced in the institute.

The activities during the year reflect the OSU site's intentions to keep people connected, minimize problems of distance, and devise ways to connect to existing or developing initiatives. Because of the growing number of in-service opportunities, the OSU WP has hired an in-service coordinator whose job is to find initiatives and groups whose purposes are compatible with work of the NWP as well as to facilitate and help shape the work of the TCs.

The activities and events developed by the OSU WP vary in length, type, and purpose. There is a book group in which teachers participate in online discussions, workshops that can be taken for graduate credit, and teacher-in-residence arrangements whereby TCs provide classroom demonstrations and coaching over time to particular schools. Some events take place at the university on Saturdays, while others are held at school sites. Media literacy is encouraged by participation in an e-journal that is organized by a TC especially knowledgeable about technology.

The breadth of the OSU WP working relationships can be seen in its connections to state initiatives as well as to professional organizations, reform groups, and individual school partnerships. These connections show the adaptation made by this site in reaching out to teachers living geographically distant from the university and finding ways to provide valuable input into state reform and improvement initiatives. The OSU WP works with the Comprehensive School Reform Demonstration Program and the State Department of Education, participates in the Oklahoma Council of Teachers of English, and has a variety of partnerships with schools and districts. In addition, it is an affiliate of the Rural Entrepreneurship Through Action Learning (REAL), an Annenberg project in which students are being exposed to skills and abilities in a microcommunity-like setting.

Recognizing problems with geographical isolation, the site works hard to expand the horizons of its TCs, sending 20 teachers to the national NWP meeting at NCTE every year. Locally, the site is serving more low-income populations than it has ever done before and, in this connection, has created a 30-hour professional development program dealing specifically with literacy development. Because of its contributions throughout the northern part of Oklahoma, and its achievements in creating TCs who are respected leaders in professional development in the state, a new site is being planned at Southwestern Oklahoma State University in Weatherford, with the help of a teacher consultant from the OSU WP.

LEADERSHIP: THE WRITING PROJECT WAY

In earlier studies of networks, leadership had always been spoken about as being facilitative and collaborative (Crandall, 1983; Lieberman & Grolnick, 1996; Parker, 1979). By studying these two sites in depth, we were able to compare leadership in the NWP to these earlier descriptions, as well as to each other. It appears that their practice confirms the past studies and that differences are a product of the different contexts of the sites and their maturity.

We observed the directors of both sites as they carried out their leadership roles during the summer institute. They both attended and participated in the institute, benefiting from experiential learning in the same way as other participants. They were at different times teacher, facilitator, broker, fund-raiser, entrepreneur, decision maker, proposal writer, organizer—and, most important, "cultural carrier" of the Writing Project way of working. In NWP terms, this means always starting any learning experience by finding out what people already know; providing a learning experience that is centered on the learner; building activities around the teachers' work; and providing for critique, feedback, and support. Directors *negotiate* and *broker* with principals, school districts, state officials, and university personnel, creating new relationships and new possibilities (e.g., the special-interest group on Advanced Placement at UCLA, or working with state-mandated programs at OSU). Directors aim at *inclusiveness*, looking to see if anyone is not being included and intervening if necessary. At these two sites much effort is given to expanding the Writing Project to underserved populations: at UCLA working with second-language learners; at OSU reaching out to poor communities that have had little access to in-service because of their isolated geographical locations. (UCLA has been a part of the Urban Sites Network, seeking to better their work in urban areas, while OSU has been a part of the federal Rural Sites Network, finding ways to connect to and better serve isolated rural areas).

Directors make a concerted effort to find teachers with *leadership potential* and provide them with *real* work to do. (For example, in our study, both directors found three teachers they thought would benefit from working with us to document the learning of selected students in their own classrooms.) They look for people to take leadership responsibilities by convening a special-interest group or a group of teacher researchers. In bringing new people into leadership positions in appropriate situations, directors bring new energy and commitment to the work of the NWP.

Districts sometimes call the NWP for help with a specific program, while, at other times, the director will become involved in helping them shape what they need. At the UCLA site the scope of the work has grown so much that the director's role has changed. Whereas at a newer site, the director leads or participates in many activities, at this mature site there are now many different leaders for numerous programs and organizational arrangements: an associate director leads one of the partnerships, a TC leads the urban initiative, another TC leads the Early Childhood Literacy group, and so forth. Many events and activities are now under the UCLA WP umbrella, and leadership by the director takes the form of facilitating, coaching, talent seeking, and negotiating, with less time spent in direct involvement with project work.

At the OSU WP, the director sees herself as an *agent*: "You're always thinking about—given this project that's coming up—who would be good at doing X? How can we get the people, the expertise, the money to support the work?" It appears that sites go through stages, and as they do, the nature of the director's work changes. In the beginning, organizing the summer institute is central to the work. Following the institute, the development of programs and activities that continue throughout the year occupies the director, for it is "real work" that keeps teachers connected beyond the summer. For example, sites are encouraged to hold conferences at which the presentation of teachers' work is the centerpiece. In the OSU WP, because of its large area, the director created four 3-day conferences at different locations throughout the site.

Both the UCLA WP and OSU WP directors describe a time during the summer institute when teachers come to understand that they are participating in a program that places their knowledge and expertise at the center. The awareness that they are both valued and respected leads some teachers to take on more responsibility. At OSU that time comes when the institute anthology is taken over by the teacher participants, and at UCLA when the teachers in writing groups realize that they are in charge of what happens in their group—that they are the experts as well as the learners.

Again, previous studies of networks have described leadership as being facilitative—playing the role of broker, finding expertise, and providing leadership opportunities (Lieberman & Grolnick, 1996). Directors in the NWP carry out these functions with an added emphasis on the development of new leadership. While working at a local site gives the TCs experience as leaders, the social practices that they participate in at the local site give substance and meaning to the role as they learn to do the following:

- "Scout talent"—looking for future leaders
- Make connections—looking for ways to connect people to one another and connect the Writing Project to other initiatives, schools, and school reform efforts
- Inspire people—encouraging teachers to take leadership, to be staff developers
- Facilitate learning possibilities—organizing learning experiences that make teachers the center of their own learning through writing groups in which teachers teach teachers
- Present new ideas using a model of collective inquiry—bringing people together as learning partners instead of presenting information with an all-knowing stance.

Directors and co-directors have many opportunities to facilitate and broker, and it appears that these ways of leading become integrated into the way they work.

SOCIAL PRACTICES AND NETWORK ORGANIZING: A KEY LESSON IN SCHOOL REFORM

The "work" of the Writing Project, first introduced during the 5-week summer invitational, brings new teachers into a culture. For large numbers of teachers, this culture provides them with inspiration, friendships, knowledge, and ways to understand their own teaching as well as its impact on their students. Understanding the social practices (see Chapter 2) that underlie this culture, as an integrated set of organizing principles, helps us to see how the work gets accomplished, how leadership is developed at the local level, and how these practices lend themselves to understanding and adaptation in different contexts. The social practices provide the framework for teachers to come together, participate in learning processes, and have opportunities to develop leadership capacities in a safe environment. Basic to the social practices is involving teachers in ways of learning that put them at the center, respecting their knowledge, connecting them to peers and practice, and giving them an opportunity to be supported by and connected to a professional community. Teachers find that they can learn, teach, lead, ask questions, write, think, be vulnerable, get inspired, be themselves both personally and professionally—and all this in a context that encourages them to rethink who they are and what they are going to do and be as teachers, learners, and leaders.

The social practices that form the basis of network building happen in the same ways, even as they are adapted to the different contexts of each site. After the invitational institute, professional development activities are organized to take place for the remainder of the year and subsequent summers. As we see from the diagrams of both sites, these take many forms. At OSU, teachers work with particular schools in a series of workshops that last for 10 weeks. At UCLA there are partnerships with several districts, each crafting their professional development programs to suit their needs, with TCs as their leaders. The various types of year-long and summer activities are framed around the needs of the site in typical network fashion. Activities are created that have relevance and resonance to the site. For example, "Writing from Day One" at UCLA attends to the problems of teachers teaching bilingual students to write, while at OSU professional development is organized around the state-mandated Comprehensive School Reform Demonstration Program as well as other individually negotiated professional development consultant arrangements.

We have stressed the idea that the social practices of the NWP provide a way of working that can be applied in different locations and contexts. Such a network arrangement, providing opportunities for the continuing growth and development of teachers, can be of great importance to our understanding of school reform. It may be that we can learn from the NWP that if professional development is to become a part of a teacher's life, it must combine not just new knowledge but a way of building new relationships within a professional community. One feeds the other, and both help teachers think differently about their own learning as well as their identity as teachers.

The next part of our study was to follow six teachers from the two sites to their classrooms to see if we could observe the influences and impact of network learning on their classroom practice.

Chapter 4

Portraits in Teaching: Connecting Network Learning, Classroom Teaching, and Student Accomplishment

As we have described in Chapters 2 and 3, we saw firsthand how the social interactions during the summer institutes built an identifiable NWP culture, infused with shared values. Moreover, the sustained growth of the NWP since its beginnings in 1974 demonstrates that the organization has been able to use a network structure for increasing membership and expanding influence. Still, we wanted to understand better *how* individual TCs shoulder the mantle of teacher leadership and bring what they learn to widening circles of colleagues. Perhaps even more important, we wanted to know whether what they told us they were learning through the NWP actually had an impact on what students experience in their classrooms.

As a result, we asked the site directors to help us locate six actively contributing TCs whose length of time in the network varied. Ultimately, we selected from each site one teacher brand-new to the network and two others who had been TCs for varying lengths of time, anywhere from 6 to 20 years. From the two novices, we wanted to know what they had learned from the summer institutes and whether and how they translated what they learned into actual practice with students and colleagues. With the veteran TCs, we explored what motivated their continued involvement, how they participated over time, and what differences, if any, their involvement made for students and colleagues.

For this chapter, we draw on field notes from our observations of the teachers working in their classrooms during the 1999–2000 schoolyear, individual and collective interviews with them, focus group interviews in which they participated, and the narratives they wrote during the second year of our study. Each of the teachers' narratives contained two sections: (1) chronological accounts of the academic progress of two to three students in their classrooms, including descriptions of teaching strategies, student work samples, and assessments of those samples, and (2) autobiographical accounts of their initial and evolving participation in the NWP, as well as how that involvement shaped their professional thinking and practice. The narratives these teachers created were robust texts, allowing us to peer into their perspectives on their participation in the NWP and how it affected their ongoing classroom practices. Furthermore, the narratives provided rich insights into how the six teachers thought about and then responded to challenges working with individual students. Coupled with our observations of their classroom teaching, the narratives fleshed out how what they learned in the NWP helped them to plan, design, structure, and carry out daily work as they confronted particular issues dealing with students.

The ways in which TCs make NWP ideas manifest in practice depend on a variety of variables: individual passions and intentions, particular students, and local contexts. Moreover, each NWP site brings its own political and economic complications to the work of the NWP. These can range from state mandates, to problems building leadership, to inadequate resources. As we watched TCs struggle to adapt their learning to local conditions and personalities, we began to understand better the complexities involved in translating professional learning into actual practice.

THE INITIATES: LAURA AND LISA

Laura and Lisa, whom we met during the summer institutes at UCLA and OSU, respectively, were both relatively new to the profession and brand-new to the NWP. Both taught in poor neighborhoods with large Spanish-speaking immigrant populations, and both worked out of an intense commitment to foster *all* children's learning. There were also clear differences, the most obvious being location. Laura taught in Los Angeles, where she dealt with a particularly fierce controversy over bilingual education. Lisa worked in a deteriorating elementary school building, situated in the outskirts of Oklahoma City, where she struggled with an increasing focus on standardized test scores. And, of course, both teachers brought their distinctive personalities and autobiographies to their work.

Laura: "I wanted it to be authentic, real, and good."

Like many teachers, Laura is both an idealist and a realist. She has deep commitments to help children learn and yet also knows she must function in a bureaucracy. Laura's core values, a mixture of this idealism and realism, poured out in our fall interview with her shortly after the summer institute initiating her into the NWP. During that interview, she described her anxiety as she had prepared the required teaching demonstration for her colleagues. The stakes seemed quite high, she explained, because she had great respect for her colleagues. As she put it, "I wanted it [the demonstration] to be authentic, real, and good." In this one simple sentence, Laura captured the essence of her pedagogical philosophy, one she had recently found to be in conflict with district policy.

The story of Laura's initiation into the NWP, followed by her first year teaching after the institute, highlights a problem that the NWP continually faces. What do TCs do when their ideas about best practices conflict directly with policy initiatives in their schools, districts, and states? Laura faced exactly such a problem in Los Angeles. A bilingual teacher who speaks fluent Spanish, Laura contends that the best way to ensure English literacy in ESL students is to allow them also to develop "academic fluency" in their first language. Discussions on this very topic during the summer institute reinforced her views and gave her new ideas for translating them into practice. As a consequence, she began the subsequent schoolyear "buzzing" with ideas and strategies. Meanwhile, however, in the back of her head, she knew that

California's recently enacted Proposition 227 would require her to prepare her students for an English-only classroom in 1 short year. At that time, she was about to start her second year of teaching second grade after 3 years of teaching kindergarten. On the one hand, Laura had been reenergized by her institute experiences. On the other, Proposition 227 threatened to cast a long shadow over her plans for the upcoming year.

Of course, Laura knew she could not ignore her responsibility to prepare students adequately for an English-only classroom. But she was unwilling simply to acquiesce to a policy she believed might constrain rather than foster her students' English literacy. After all, she had made some sacrifices to be able to do what she believed was right for her students. In order to attend the institute, she had sacrificed her routine summer escape from "hot and trafficky" Los Angeles. And she had done so, in part, because she wanted to work with a community of teachers to figure out ways to deal with Proposition 227.

In sum, the institute did not do much to change Laura's basic teaching philosophy. She already knew writing can and should be a way for students to express and share themselves, to make sense of new learning, and to find relevant connections between what they learn and their own lives. What the institute *did* do for Laura was to legitimate these values and equip her with multiple strategies and resources to carry them out in her classroom. In addition, it gave her firsthand experience with how immersion in the processes and sharing of writing builds strong learning communities.

The lessons she learned from the institute about teacher learning gave her the courage to ask an administrator in her building to give her "a whole day [during the fall in-service] to share activities and ideas from my Writing Project experience." She wrote later:

> The best part about the day was the amount of writing we did as a staff. People I never expected to be writers shared beautiful things, unlikely groups of teachers actually worked together to write a song or a poem, and everyone had a chance through the activities to not only be a teacher of writing but to be a WRITER.

Thus, within only weeks of the institute, Laura brought back to her school three key NWP notions: a sense of professional responsibility to share new ideas with colleagues, a commitment to build professional community through writing, and the belief that the teaching of writing improves when teachers engage in the *practice* of writing.

Once the students were back in the building, however, her enthusiasm flagged. All but four of her students spoke Spanish as a first language. At first, she tried out a few NWP ideas, but one question kept dogging her: In 9 short months, was she really going to have these children prepared to enter an English-only third grade? Out of desperation, she found herself turning to repetitive cycles of recitations and drills in English vocabulary and mechanics.

Very quickly, the faces of her students revealed signs of trouble. In Laura's words, "the kids seemed to be going on auto-pilot." She remembered later, "They were going to follow along and do what everyone else did" in order to please her and "avoid risks." Soon afterward, she decided she could no longer bear their mechanical, joyless expressions. NWP ideas, she said, "just came back," giving her a context to recall the "philosophy I had about my students being themselves writers." If students' learning was to be "authentic, real, and good," she knew that she was going to have to work with them to build a learning community safe enough for risk taking and public sharing. It wasn't that Laura discounted the role of memorization, repetition, and drill. In fact, she had students doing some of all three. But she wanted a broader range of possibilities for them.

She held a brief pow-wow with a fellow second-grade teacher who agreed to take her four native English speakers during language arts; in exchange, Laura took her colleague's ESL students. She set up an "author's chair" at the front of her room and allowed the students choices in what they wrote and read. She paired them up for book talks, created time for silent reading, and instituted writing workshops. In addition, she taught them how to use computers for drafting, revision, and publication. Convinced that their command of English would only come with a sense of safety and confidence, she allowed those particularly reticent in English to speak and write in Spanish first until they gained some confidence. Eventually, she introduced them to compelling experiences with writing and speaking in Spanish and then eased them into translating their thoughts into English. In other words, she strengthened the children's Spanish literacy and then used it to scaffold English instruction.

Although Proposition 227 was designed to deny these very options, Laura had found the courage to choose them anyway. During the preceding summer institute, she had participated in discussions and demonstrations about how to live with Proposition 227 without forfeiting what she believed. Then she continued these conversations during the schoolyear within her building and with colleagues across the district. While not wanting simply to capitulate to the demands of Proposition 227, she also didn't want to set her second-graders up for failure. She had to find a third way.

The author's chair, perhaps more than anything in her classroom, symbolizes Laura's alternative approach. As she put it:

> I personally experienced how scary it is to be a writer, to share your work in the author's chair, and then to lay out your work to be critiqued by your peers. I also learned what it was like to really trust a group of people with a story I had written. We laughed and cried . . . and wrote and wrote and wrote. For the first time, I experienced the true need to write, a craving to put the pen to paper long after class was over. I feel that this was essential to my growth as a person, and I know that I wanted to be able to provide a similar experience for my own students.

Through daily use of the author's chair with students, Laura nudged them toward increasing use of English without stripping them of confidence. In her attempts to make writing "authentic," she invited students to write about their families, their problems on the playground, their unique perceptions of the natural world, their opinions about books. In her attempt to make writing "real" for them, she provided them with audiences about whom they cared—their peers, their parents, and their principal. In her attempt to make writing "good," she incorporated minilessons in spelling and mechanics and required them to pass muster with peers, revise, and "publish" on the computer or classroom walls.

Laura told us about a breakthrough event, a public celebration of writing, when her students read poems to their mothers in both English and Spanish. She accounted for her students' success this way:

> But looking back on it now, I realize that it was not just that Mother's Day poetry lesson that enabled my students to share their writing at such a ceremonious event. It wasn't like I had just decided to teach "Writing Project–style" on that one occasion. That poetry reading was possible for my students because I had been living, teaching, and implementing Writing Project ideas since September. All of that time in author's chair, all of those poems we learned and imitated, all of the prewrites and cooperative learning brainstorming, all of the Venn diagrams, and the countless hours editing and revising at the computer lab had helped my students in their journey to become writers. All of the journal entries, science journals, math journals, social studies journals, vacation journals, and creative writing homework—all of these things were necessary building blocks. Above all, I felt that creating an atmosphere of trust and support was crucial. Having a safe place to take risks helped my students to grow in their self-confidence and to realize the importance of writing in all aspects of their lives.

Lisa: "Leading students through a learning experience that worked for me"

Lisa, unlike Laura, was less certain about her teaching philosophy. In fact, there were times before her involvement in the NWP when she felt torn in two ideological directions. Having served in the military before becoming a teacher, Lisa had learned from experience that a strictly disciplined environment *can* build confidence.

Self-esteem, she tended to believe, evolves from academic success and good behavior more frequently than it produces them. In keeping with this position, she instituted a Disciplinary Committee in her elementary school. Children who repeatedly broke school rules were required to appear with their parents before the committee to discuss the problem, receive appropriate sanctions, and seek solutions. Most children tried to avoid this experience.

Although Lisa affirmed the value of consistent and fair discipline, her own troubled childhood had taught her that children often need more. Lisa spent her girlhood reading and writing, finding solace in her journal and in her books. Here and there, she encountered an adult, usually a teacher, who nurtured her talents and made her feel smart. In retrospect, she viewed her childhood habits of reading and writing, her encounters with supportive adults, and the discipline and structure she gained from the military as just the right combination. Learners, including her students, she concluded, need strong literacy skills, good relationships with their teachers, and a structured environment in which to learn self-discipline. But confronted with instances of student misbehavior or low achievement, she would waffle about which of these to stress. Should she take firm disciplinary action or lend a sympathetic ear?

After the institute, Lisa was able to replace this troubling ambivalence with a more satisfying synthesis. She had seen during the institute that high academic expectations are not necessarily opposed to empathy and community building. The institute itself had become for her a strong, nurturing community that also provided the best possible structure for serious, intense learning. Lisa explained why: "You're with all these people and they all have such good ideas and they're really interested in what you think. It makes you proud to be a teacher and anxious to learn as much as you can." The institute also taught her that teachers, as learners, are far more motivated if they take ownership over the shape and direction of learning. Why wouldn't all these conditions also support her students' learning? Mulling this over, she recalled the many drills she had marched her students through the previous schoolyear and winced.

When we followed Lisa into her fourth-grade classroom after the institute, we recognized the NWP's impact on her immediately. Children's creative writing and artwork perked up dreary taupe walls, and children clustered in small groups pursuing a variety of tasks. At different junctures, we saw students rehearsing scenes from stories, engaged in "book talks" with reading buddies, listening to Lisa reading aloud, reading each other's writing and commenting on it, choosing their own books for silent reading, writing about their reading, generating their own topics for personal writing, drafting at computers, and recording words in their own personalized "spelling books."

For a special week in the late spring of that year, Lisa set up pup tents in her classroom. To simulate the outdoors, she played recordings of rushing streams, chirping crickets, and singing birds. At intervals, children moved from tent to tent—each one a station with assignments in drawing, writing, and/or reading. Lisa explained later that she had heard during the summer institute about writing camps for children sponsored by the OSU Writing Project. She knew that few, if any, of her students' families could afford children's summer camps and that it might take a while to find the funding for such a camp in her own school or district. So she decided to create an experience that would give her students the flavor of what it might be like to go to camp while stimulating their reading and writing skills in the process.

Despite Lisa's many enthusiasms, she could also be quite skeptical. Before becoming a believer in any teaching approach, no matter how well recommended, she looked for demonstrable evidence that it had the capacity to improve students' learning. Ideological arguments seldom impressed her. Quite the opposite, in fact. Listening to the array of opinions expressed by respected colleagues during the summer institute, Lisa decided that good teachers need to be "flexibilists," a term she coined. For an OSU newsletter she wrote an essay explaining what she meant. She argued that teachers ought to let go of ideological orthodoxy and actively search for what's best for their students. "I don't want to fall into a category," she said during an interview. "I don't want to just say that this is my philosophy and then just stick with that. . . . I need to look at *everything* to help kids' learning." Lisa claimed that the summer institute, by engaging her in critical reading, reflection, and dialogue and by introducing her to teacher research, gave her ways to explore her options systematically and to make better choices.

Although Lisa was skeptical of standardized tests, she was also skeptical of arguments that too easily dismiss them. She considered tests "just one more source of information to tell you how your students were doing." Nevertheless, she wanted other measures to accompany them, especially about aspects of students' learning that typically elude test questions. In this spirit, Lisa began painstakingly collecting samples of student work, placing them in portfolios, and keeping careful charts of reading and writing test scores. For her work with us, she tracked three students particularly closely and generated categories to assess their work based in part on district standards for reading and writing skills. These included a range of writing composition skills (writing a paragraph, using punctuation, developing a story, writing a letter, and so forth) and reading comprehension skills (understanding characters, seeing cause and effect, using context clues, and so forth). Her approach was to embed and assess these skills in more holistic reading and writing assignments. At the end of the year, she weighed her overall evaluations against her students' scores on district tests. The tests confirmed Lisa's judgment. Her students had made marked, demonstrable progress in reading and writing and exceeded her district's most optimistic projections.

Lisa claimed she owed this success to what she had learned during the institute. She wrote in her narrative, "I tested my courage and looked at each child as an individual, following a plan of learning to write by writing, learning to read by reading, and connecting the two." Moreover, she contended that her students had learned to work hard without forfeiting the fun in learning, and though they were allowed individual choices, they could still meet high expectations. Perhaps most important for Lisa, her students had learned to read and write through the actual *processes* of reading and writing. She explained:

I tend to tackle challenges by way of questions, and I began this schoolyear with several in mind. Could I transfer the Writing Project experience to the classroom? Could I prove that students could conquer district-mandated skills through reading and writing (as opposed to worksheet exercises and drills)? Would connecting reading and writing to the lives of children motivate them to read and write? Reflecting on the schoolyear and the work of these three students, I could simply reply, "Yes, yes, yes." . . . Children became writers and lovers of books. They transferred language skills to other content areas. They learned to express their thoughts and feelings for the sake of assessment, for the sake of communication, and just as important, for fun.

BECOMING TEACHER LEADERS: MARLENE AND MARY

When we asked Marlene and Mary about the value of their participation in the NWP, both stressed their evolving roles as leaders. For Marlene, playing a leadership role was especially important because she wanted to have an influence on what happened to students of color in classrooms. For Mary, becoming a TC meant having the opportunity to demonstrate for colleagues how to provide students with a sound background in grammar, mechanics, and reading composition skills without interrupting reading and writing as pleasurable, meaningful activities. For both, the NWP transformed how they thought about their roles and responsibilities as professionals, extending both beyond the walls of their classrooms. They became teachers of teachers.

Marlene: "I'm feeling empowered as a teacher to say that maybe I do know something about how students best learn."

Like many new teachers in their first teaching job, Marlene, who worked in Los Angeles, quickly became acclimated to the teaching style predominant among the veteran teachers in her building. At that time, she taught in a relatively affluent, "mostly White" suburban high school almost 30 miles from her home. She was one of very few teachers of color in the building. She described the prevailing approach as "traditional." When we asked what she meant by that, she said, "You know, where you *assign* writing rather than teaching it." According to Marlene, teachers approached writing instruction by assigning topics, establishing due dates, and providing feedback only on finished products. Opportunities for instruction during the process of writing, including revision, were nonexistent. She described teaching, in accordance with that approach, as a yearly, free-standing "10-week grammar unit." The idea was to front-load mechanics and punctuation instruction and then expect students to transfer what they had learned into their writing.

In the beginning, Marlene was relatively comfortable with all this. Ultimately, however, a series of circumstances converged to unsettle her. First, she was increasingly troubled by students in her remedial courses for whom "the traditional approach" wasn't working. Second, she had decided to transfer to another high school—her own alma mater—located in the neighborhood where she had grown up and continued to live. There, the majority of the students were African American, although there was a growing Hispanic population. "I knew it wasn't going to be the same, knowing that I would teach different kinds of students." Third, she had a growing concern about the disproportionate number of African American students who become alienated and resistant in public schools. Starved for resources and strategies that would help her make the transition from a traditional school, where she already felt she had failed to meet some students' needs, to her own alma mater, where she would most certainly face more challenges, she signed up for a series of workshops led by a TC:

> The workshops were after school and each time we had a different thing we talked about. She [the TC] would have presenters in. . . . And they would show us various writing strategies and I would go back and try one. I think the I-Search paper is the one that really caught my attention.

When we asked her why the I-Search strategy was important, she said, "Instead of doing research just with books, students need to be very involved in a lot of primary research where they have to talk to an expert and write away for information or call people, so that it's not just a library kind of assignment." In preparation for her move to her alma mater, she tried out an I-Search assignment with her remedial classes in her current high school, where, according to Marlene, "it was very successful." She explained, "I think because I wasn't locked into a traditional research paper, the students picked topics that I probably wouldn't have accepted before." Students, who had become enervated by worksheets and drills, pursued their research with relish, thoroughness, and creativity, she contended.

The next year, having begun teaching at her alma mater, Marlene's thirst for more NWP strategies intensified. Within months, she received an invitation to apply to the summer institute and leaped at it. The experience proved anything but disappointing. The writing instruction modeled during the institute decoded "the mystery of good writing," unpacking the process. This, she believed, was exactly what some of her students would need as they struggled to become writers. We asked her to describe how she took her students through the writing process:

> First, there's going to be some prewriting, and that could
> be anything from reading a story to having a discussion to
> doing some brainstorming, clustering, mapping, all of that.
> You're going to organize your thoughts. . . . Then you
> move on to drafting, and we try to do that quickly and not
> belabor the point. Sit down and write. Get it down. Then
> bring it back, and we're going to sit in small groups and do
> some kind of sharing. We needed to talk about how to
> share because some people weren't used to sharing. How
> do you share? Don't just look for spelling errors. . . . We
> talked about the difference between revising and editing,
> so they could talk more about clarifying ideas versus doing
> all the editing things too early in the process. We talked
> about the fact that real writers really often do many drafts.

Though she would not claim overnight success for all of her students, she did say that her students showed:

> more engagement. You know, I can't say they were always excited. I wish I *could* say they were always excited. I had some people who love to write, and they come bubbling in with their drafts and win contests, but for a lot of people, it's just getting over the idea that they can't write.

For some students, Marlene argued, simply putting pen to paper in a purposeful way and producing something on paper amounted to a breakthrough. When we observed Marlene in action, she worked actively to build classroom community so students would support one another's learning. For one particular unit, the students wrote step-by-step, how-to descriptions and then gave demonstrations. Topics ranged from making egg salad to pursuing a hobby. Consequently, students learned a great deal *about* as well as *from* one another. Marlene also continued to unpack intellectual processes for them. For one lesson, she discussed how dictionaries are constructed, asking students to think of words from street slang as exemplars for discerning meanings. As they did, she and the students reversed roles: She became the learner and they the teachers, defining words for her or challenging her to guess meanings through context clues.

On another day, she gave students the acronym SOAPS to help them remember dimensions of speech making: subject, occasion, audience, purpose, and speaker. According to Marlene, in order to get some high school students writing, teachers need to pique their interest with a wide range of relevant and engrossing adolescent literature, scaffold the processes, and provide them with engaging classroom activities. The NWP network provided, on an ongoing basis, a wealth of resources for doing all three.

Marlene began her NWP participation eager to learn "a lot of different strategies." She left it not only having met that goal but also with a vision of herself as a leader, a watershed moment in her career. For her first 8 years of teaching, working in the suburbs, she had been among the youngest of the faculty. No one asked for her advice; they gave it. She learned to look to others for answers. The institute, however, succeeded in releasing her accumulating knowledge and experience. When she gave her demonstration, she began to see that "maybe I *do* know something about how students best learn." She began to see why and how she could become a teacher of teachers.

And a teacher of teachers she has become. Over the 12 years she has been a TC, Marlene's leadership roles have evolved, expanding beyond her school and district to state and national levels. She has given teaching demonstrations for teachers inside and outside the NWP. At the time of our research, Marlene served on the advisory board of the UCLA site and facilitated teacher research and study groups. Eventually, she worked at both state and national levels on projects focusing particularly on "urban issues and teacher research."

While the NWP helped her recognize and express what she had learned from her own practice, the organization also enabled her to recognize knowledge she did *not* have. Thus, she was inspired to "become a regular reader again" of educational literature. Marlene captured NWP influences this way:

> I learned if I'm a teacher of writing I have to be a writer. . . .
> If I'm going to be a teacher of reading, I have to be a reader.
> . . . Then the next step was I need to share my teaching
> with other people and not be afraid to do that. And to
> know that I do have some good ideas that other people
> would like to hear about. . . . And I think another transfor-
> mation was becoming a teacher-researcher. And that helped
> me to gain this inquiring stance into what I do and to keep
> looking for answers when things aren't going right, to try
> to look at some evidence or data to figure it out.

We know Marlene continues to wrestle with questions about how to effectively teach the students whom public schools seem continually to fail. But she says the NWP has provided invaluable support as she searches for answers. She has a network of knowledgeable colleagues, opportunities and strategies to share what she has learned, and the knowledge and skills to conduct systematic inquiry into problems of practice. In the end, she insists that the NWP has made her believe in herself as a thinker, a writer, and a leader and that the same should be done for students in public school classrooms.

Mary: "The greatest opportunity has been to present my ideas to other teachers."

During her first few years teaching, Mary made significant accomplishments as a writing teacher. As a student teacher, she learned about writing workshops from her cooperating teacher, which she incorporated into her own classroom once she became a full-time teacher. She began developing portfolio assessments of student writing and co-chaired her district's Language Arts Committee. While doing all this, she also earned a master of arts degree in Teaching Writing. By the time Mary moved to Oklahoma, her commitment to writing instruction had become a passion. She landed a teaching position in a multiage classroom, and a colleague placed an application to the OSU summer institute in her mailbox. She applied immediately.

Mary wanted to attend for several reasons. In her first assignment as a teacher, she felt pressure to give up her workshop approach in order to cover all the English "skills" many of the tenured teachers had declared essential. From that experience, she learned how isolated a teacher can feel without supportive colleagues. Thus, she looked forward to spending time "writing, learning, and sharing ideas with teachers who value writing in the classroom." Second, not only did she want affirmation for her hard-won approach, she also wanted to expose other teachers to it. She found it especially appealing that teachers had opportunities "to develop effective workshops to share ideas with colleagues." And finally, she hoped that networking with other teachers participating in the OSU region would help her get to know her newly adopted state.

Mary had not fully anticipated, however, the jitters she would feel sharing writing with colleagues, and this became a source of significant collateral learning. She wrote about her first experience:

The butterflies in my stomach began to flutter, and I hoped my group would like my writing. I read my piece about the log cabin my dad and grandfather had built. My voice shook as I read but became less shaky as my group laughed about the flying squirrel episode and sighed when I read about the cabin being torn down. When I finished, there was silence, and then helpful comments and suggestions about how to improve my piece followed. I was encouraged and felt good about myself as a writer.

For the first time, Mary actually consciously *experienced* in a professional development setting what it felt like to be a learner. She wrote:

I think educators often forget what it was like to be a student—afraid of not having the right answer, afraid of being called stupid, or, in my case, when I participated in the summer institute, afraid of not having "good enough" writing to share.

This experience, however, eventually corroborated her belief that peer audiences provide a powerful impetus for writers to stretch and improve.

Having her convictions affirmed proved to be a double-edged sword. On the one hand, her knowledge and enthusiasm grew. On the other, her frustrations also mounted. Two years after the institute, she faced, along with the standardized "testing tidal wave," a particularly exasperating schedule, which allowed only 2 hours for language arts and social studies—and even that time was fragmented into 30- to 45-minute periods throughout the schoolday. Moreover, she had to cope with students being pulled out for a variety of programs. Mary told us, "There were many days that I felt overwhelmed and unsuccessful as a teacher."

While her institute experiences instilled a vision for what literacy instruction ought to be like, the NWP had also given her strategies for negotiating and coping with frustrating realities. When we visited her classroom, we witnessed the problems she described. Students were pulled out of class. Intense discussions were interrupted by bells signaling schedule shifts. Nevertheless, Mary dealt with all of these problems by following a central NWP precept: Turn students' learning over to them. During one very brief 30-minute block of time, with very little direction, students gathered their writing folders, found assigned "buddies," chose a spot in the classroom or in the hall outside, and began sharing drafts.

We listened to several of these dyads. They stayed on-task, asked clarifying questions or requested more detail, gave each other encouragement and appreciation, and made suggestions for changes. The students seemed to be able to use even truncated amounts of time in a focused and effective way. When pulled-out students returned to the class, they knew exactly how to reengage seamlessly. One day, we watched her efficiently give a 15-minute "minilesson" focused on punctuation rules, which included opportunities for application and practice, and then move on to placing students in writing groups. Here and there, a student consulted with Mary about specific writing problems.

Mary claimed that the NWP taught her how important it is to convey to students the "real purposes" for reading and writing. For Mary, that meant helping students to "see the connections between what they want to do in their own lives and how reading and writing can help them." Writing, according to Mary, is essentially a vehicle to make the writer's ideas manifest and comprehensible to an audience. With this in mind, Mary instituted a book-making project in her sixth-grade class. She invited her students to write a story for younger children, to illustrate it and make it into a book, and then to actually read the book to second-graders in the school. Finally, they would enter their books in a contest, sponsored by a corporation.

The students took to the project eagerly, and riding on their enthusiasm, Mary slipped in a whole array of academic lessons on narrative movements, word choice (especially using active verbs), punctuation, and grammar. Because they were "publishing," the students took their work through painstaking revisions. In the end, one of her students was named a finalist in the contest. Perhaps more important, they had all seen the rapt, appreciative faces of the second-graders to whom they read their stories.

Because it was important for Mary to have "ongoing support" while she struggled with her fragmented schedule and the pressures of testing, she assumed that other teachers might require the same. This motivated her to play a particularly active role as a TC. She remembered how much the right learning conditions matter not only to students but also to teachers:

> The Writing Project offers many educational opportunities to its interested TCs. It allows teachers to be leaders in their field and have a voice in education. One of the greatest opportunities I have received as a TC is presenting my ideas to other teachers because it has helped me to become a better teacher. About 1 year after my attendance at the summer institute, I was asked to develop a workshop on minilessons, teaching skills within the context of student writing. "Sure," I agreed, knowing that I had my work cut out for me. Yes, I had been teaching writing conventions within the context of student writing, but I had nothing to share in presentable form. I was forced to take a closer look at what I was doing and why. I read books . . . looking for research to support my approach, so other teachers would believe in what I was doing. I not only found support for what I was doing, but I learned new creative ideas to try in my classroom.

Teaching other teachers requires deep and ongoing professional learning. The NWP not only empowered Mary to share her expertise, it also ensured continued professional development for *her*.

THE VETERANS: SIDONIE AND LINDA

Sidonie and Linda were the two veterans, having been in the NWP longer than the other teachers we studied from their sites. It was particularly difficult to extract from them how the NWP had influenced them. While Laura and Lisa, with their institute experiences still fresh, could articulate direct connections between what they had learned in the NWP and changes in their practices,

Sidonie and Linda could no longer distinguish NWP influences from their own thinking. As Linda put it, "I can't tell the difference anymore between my own ideas and those I've gotten from the NWP." The ideas, she told us, "get into the marrow of your bones."

Sidonie: "It was the quality of the scholarship that brought me back to the Writing Project at every opportunity—and the opportunities were plentiful."

At the time of our study, Sidonie taught with a colleague in a first- and second-grade combination classroom in a year-round school in Los Angeles. When we visited her classroom, we met her class, a highly diverse group of 40 students, busily working at centers scattered throughout the room. Seemingly self-directed, they variously worked at computers, in small groups with their teachers, at buddy reading, and at a puppet theater. At one point, after journal writing, Sidonie called on students to "go to your jobs." Immediately, one student began passing out books; another dropped a pillow on the floor, where she began reading; and another took her place at a computer. Some gathered around Sidonie, who demonstrated how to view crystal formations under a microscope. Other groups worked at a science center or on dictation and spelling. As children completed their work, they went to a roster and checked out of one activity in order to enter the next.

Besides orchestrating all this activity, Sidonie was also engaged in yet another kind of teaching. She was instructing a brand-new teacher in how to set up a busy, multicentered classroom without generating chaos. As she did, she was also socializing her new colleague into a number of specific NWP practices, such as giving students choices and engaging them in collaborative learning. Such practices, Sidonie believes, deepen children's literacy skills while making them responsible for their own learning. Moreover, Sidonie had decided to recommend this teacher to the upcoming UCLA Writing Project institute.

By the time we met Sidonie, it had been 11 years since she had attended her summer institute. For her, as for the others, the institute provided a fountain of ideas and strategies, and it initiated her into a professional learning community. But perhaps even more important for her, the institute inspired her to become a scholar of teaching in her own right. She gave us this impression of her institute experience:

> The 20 of us were not expected after 5 weeks to bring away new teaching ideas. We were expected to develop new ideas about our own teaching, the purpose and efficacy thereof, and determine if and how those ideas could be shared with other educators.

Sidonie saw the teaching demonstrations not simply as a vehicle for "swapping ideas." She saw them as a chance for "the presenter to determine why her strategy worked, how it fit into her philosophy of teaching, to what degree it was representative of a particular theoretical stance toward education, and to what level of proficiency she applied it." In other words, Sidonie valued teaching demonstrations because they afforded opportunities for reflecting on practice and bridging practice and theory.

After the institute, participation in the NWP bestowed multiple occasions for Sidonie to keep intellectually alive. She attended outreach workshops and continuity meetings, both as participant and facilitator. She led several workshop series for teachers outside the NWP and returned to summer institutes as a presenter and coleader. She participated in "working groups," formed "to study topics from technology to teaching in urban settings." Inspired by one of the latter gatherings, she began the UCLA Writing Project Early Literacy Research Group in 1996.

Sidonie wrote that the NWP helps teachers develop analytic frames for looking at their work:

> The following issues are present in every workshop, institute, and meeting. How do students best learn? How do we know students have learned? What does the teacher need to provide to promote learning? What does the teacher need to be (teacher, coach, fellow learner) if she is to ensure that learning takes place?

She argued that, rather than positioning teachers as "perennial novices," as most typical in-service models seem to do, the NWP treated teachers as "seasoned scholars."

We witnessed Sidonie's scholarship in action as she worked with one of her first-grade students, a boy who had been recommended for a special education classroom. Sidonie had talked the powers-that-be into allowing her to give the child a chance in her multiage classroom, knowing she would have a chance to work with him for 2 years. Sidonie, who had developed considerable expertise observing and documenting children's academic progress, began following him closely. She discerned his particular interests and diagnosed his weaknesses. She assessed his temperament in order to judge when to lay off and when to push.

When she recognized that he had relatively little experience with books and could only "recognize three uppercase letters by name and none by sound," she knew they both had a great deal of work to accomplish if he was going to stay out of a special education classroom. Her first move was to add time to his learning day, a 1-hour daily tutoring session, which was "a fixture" of Sidonie's literacy program. As he struggled to learn to read, her student's energy occasionally flagged in discouragement. Sidonie worked hard to preserve his dignity, but she also pushed him forward. In her narrative, she captured this struggle:

> There were alternately tears, shrugs, sighs, and very reluctant smiles. With every insistent demand I made upon him when he wanted to quit, I knew I risked making reading an unpleasant act. I also knew that if I did not take this risk, reading might be something David would want to do but would not be able to do. So every sharp order was followed with sharp praise and every refusal of sympathy was paired with an unconditional expectation of success.

Painstakingly over the next 2 years, Sidonie brought all of her NWP learning to the project of helping this child to read. Her hard work paid off. By the end of his second-grade year, not only had he learned to read, but he was reading at the third-grade level.

A sad epilogue followed this happy ending, however. Although Sidonie was convinced that the multiage approach gave children the extended time and relationships they need to build a solid literacy foundation, the administration in her school "dismantled every multiage classroom in deference to the district language arts basal and mathematics textbook adoptions." This served as an impetus for Sidonie to quit teaching and begin graduate studies. We are relieved to report, however, that Sidonie could not leave teaching for long. At the time of this writing, she had returned and was teaching ninth-grade English in another district.

Linda: "I want them to read and write and speak and listen, not just for a job, but for their lives."

Like Marlene, Linda's first exposure to the NWP came through a series of workshops led by a TC who had attended a summer institute at Oklahoma University. OSU had yet to open its site. This was in the early 1980s, shortly after Linda's three children had all reached school age and she had begun teaching. The TC was a colleague of Linda's in her high school. Remembering back to those workshops, Linda said, "Now I recognize that she followed the National Writing Project's model." Linda wrote further impressions of the workshops:

> She [the TC] arranged for food to keep our bodies as satisfied as our teaching spirits. She lined up excellent presenters who talked about and then modeled things for us, which were new to me, like the writing process, keeping journals, and teachers writing for themselves in order to be better writing teachers.

Linda went on to describe how institute fellows encountered challenging literature, worked in writing groups, compiled an anthology of their writing, and taught one another. The experience was compelling for her: "I knew from that first taste that the thinking and the environment of the Writing Project was certainly something to come back to in my professional growth." But with three young children at home and with no NWP site nearby, she knew that attending the summer institute "would just have to wait."

By 1994 the OSU site was open and running, and Linda was ready to be a fellow. She was already heavily involved in the professional development of language arts teachers in her district. One initiative, which she helped design and implement, had established standards for writing, assessment rubrics, and recommended practices for writing instruction, including the workshop approach. As a consequence, Linda went to the summer institute with a dual perspective. She continued to teach high school English, so she was looking for ideas and strategies to use with students, but she also wanted to learn effective approaches to professional development. She put it this way: "I wanted to be a better writer and a better teacher of writing, but I was even more focused on being an effective facilitator for other teachers of writing." Her epiphany came when she realized that learning to write, learning to teach others to write, and learning to teach teachers all required the same processes. She claimed, "On all three levels, the needs of learners are the same!"

When we pressed Linda to describe those needs, she struggled to remember back to the institute. First, she said, "I think one of the most important things for me was the awareness that we are all in different places professionally and that's okay." She discovered through the institute that learners always come with different experiences, abilities, and interests and need to be accepted for who and where they are. They also need to be treated as if they have something of value to say to others. When we visited Linda's classroom, we saw her placing students in small groups where each member of the group had a serious role to play. Together, they worked to find meaning in literature, like *The Most Dangerous Game* or *The Prince*, or to provide feedback on one another's writing. No student was "left off the hook."

Second, Linda contended that learning requires reflection. Because of her participation in the NWP, she "came across teacher lore, that is, teachers writing about experiences in the classroom, even the idea of writing-to-learn." She said the institute taught her that this practice deepens teachers' capacities for self-critique. Recognizing that students in classrooms could benefit from this same sort of reflection, she helped create new district guidelines for in-class opportunities at writing-to-learn. And she asked her own students increasingly to write about their experiences as learners.

Third, Linda explained, learners need to take ownership over their own learning. If teachers are really going to engage in professional learning, she contended, then they need to "own" both what they already know and what they have yet to know in order to be better teachers. She claimed it was the same for students. Learning should connect to what students already know, but it should also align with what students think they "need to know." In fact, when we visited her high school, we saw her students deliver minilessons focused on grammar and punctuation errors that many of them were making.

Linda demonstrated how much this notion of ownership mattered to her when she described a boy in her class who was a particular challenge:

> He is very much the teacher pleaser. If I ask him to do it, he wants to do it. And not for the grade; it's not just that. He wants to please *me*. He respects me; he respects the teacher's role. I have a hard time getting him to tell me what he *really* thinks. He is such a good student, but I want to move him away from being a teacher pleaser, so he can be autonomous and independent. I want him to learn for his own sake, for his own purposes. Once in a while I hear him break into his own voice, but most of the time he just wants to please. . . . One time, though, he really argued about something. It was great.

There is a price to be paid, however, for shifting control to the students, and Linda sometimes struggled with that:

> Kids now [after she joined the NWP] are more frustrated with my teaching than they used to be. Things used to be very clear-cut for me and for them. But I've changed a lot,

and sometimes the kids are not on the same page with me even though I think I know what I'm doing. Half of my teaching day, for instance, I spend with honors kids, and they can be so traditional. And they want to know what I want and they want to do it right. And I had a conference with a parent, and it was all about how I grade. It was fine in the end, but I realize I'm frustrating to people. It's not like everything's rosy.

She explained that teachers who want recipes could also become temporarily frustrated with the professional development approaches she designs. Wrestling with how much direction and inspiration to provide learners without making them dependent continued to be an issue for her.

Finally, Linda talked about the importance of learners seeing the connection between what they learn and what they want to accomplish in the world. When we asked her what she wanted bottom-line for her students, she said, "I want them to read and write and speak and listen, not just for a job, but for their lives." She wanted to provide professional development opportunities for teachers, like the one she had during the summer institute, where teachers are approached "as thinking individuals with expertise to offer," as well as individuals with areas of interest and concerns to pursue to make them better teachers. Linda's professional learning through the NWP was completely entangled with her professional challenges—so much so that she told us:

It's so hard for me to figure out what comes first. Do I get ideas and issues from the Writing Project and then move those locally; or do I get the questions locally and then go to the writing project for answers?

During our study, Linda was traveling one Sunday a month—a 45-minute trip each way—to meet two of her NWP colleagues, also high school English teachers, at Willie's café, a meeting place in a small town (Seiling, Oklahoma) equidistant from their respective homes. One Sunday, we joined the group and met Rebecca, one of the "Seiling Sunday teachers." She was a new TC, having attended the institute only 2 years before, and worked in a tiny, rural high school where she taught English to kids at every grade level. When I asked Linda why making such a long trip was worth it to her—especially on a weekend—she said, "Rebecca is really the reason we started this. The last meeting of the institute she was almost in tears saying, 'I need this kind of support, this kind of help.'" Then she added, "Gatherings like these replicate the institute. You're working with people that are already good and already committed, and you get so many ideas and so much support from one another." Then the three turned back to their discussion about effective writing assignments.

THE COMMON GROUND

We followed these six teachers closely because we wanted to know whether their learning in the NWP network actually made its way to their classrooms. For all six, it clearly had. We saw echoes of the summer institutes as we followed them into their classrooms, both in the strategies they used and in the ways in which they interacted with students and colleagues.

Although each of these teachers had an individual style and a unique set of challenges, they shared some common convictions. First, they were deeply committed to students' literacy and believed in the power of writing-to-learn. Second, each created classroom communities, capable of both critique and support, as an essential context for learning.

They created these communities by enacting the same social practices that had built strong communities among their colleagues in the NWP. This allowed them to focus on community without sublimating individual needs and interests. They treated their students as if each of them had something valuable to contribute to one another and then engaged them in peer teaching. They created opportunities for their students to make their ideas and writing public. They worked hard to give them ownership over their own learning. They designed the learning environment so that students could learn-by-doing and learn-in-relationship. By providing students choices and building on their interests and needs, they provided an array of entry points to engage in learning. They encouraged students to reflect on their own learning and yet encouraged them to participate in the learning of others.

As each faced what she saw as a core struggle to practice what she had learned from the NWP in the face of local and political constraints, they all reached out to colleagues within the NWP network and beyond. When they took the role of teaching other teachers, they stayed faithful to the model and enacted the social practices they had learned in the institutes. They stayed committed to professional learning by attending continuity workshops and professional conferences, participating in online discussions, collaborating informally, and/or gathering at writing retreats. In all these ways, they scattered seeds for improving teaching practices and expanding NWP influence. And in all these ways, they consistently gathered the courage, despite sometimes daunting obstacles, to persist in doing what they felt was best for student learning.

Chapter 5

The National Writing Project: Its Challenges and Contributions

Getting "inside the National Writing Project" by studying two sites helped us understand its complicated, multilayered structure, giving us insights into effective professional development in general and the functioning of the NWP in particular. The 5-week institute, the development and support of teacher consultants, the creation and expansion of a year-long program, the continuous involvement and shaping of local and national agendas, and the building of a local Writing Project culture produce the complex layers of this network. Moreover, because this is a national network, it requires reciprocal and ongoing connections between and among local sites and the national office.

Successful networks draw people together from disparate contexts around shared purposes and work, and yet they still retain the ability to stay close to the local needs of their members. They are, in other words, inherently flexible. The work of the NWP, for instance, emerges from needs embedded in local contexts, and yet it manages to sustain a national, cohesive identity. Moreover, each individual site must negotiate its own school–university partnership, often a difficult task. Tensions inevitably arise, however, and, for the NWP, these revolve around questions of quality control, decentralization, school–university partnerships, and the network's ability to occupy a "third space" (Lieberman & Grolnick, 1996).

NETWORK WAY OF ORGANIZING:
CHALLENGES AND ADAPTATIONS

A major problem of all decentralized organizations, and networks in particular, is the problem of quality control. It is generally accepted that local work—work that involves teachers in improving their own classrooms—is the best hope for changing what happens in classrooms. But how do we know that teachers are really using new and improved practices? And how do we know whether the practices that teachers learn lead to enhanced student learning and accomplishment?

For our study, we developed two strategies to try to answer these questions. First, we followed three teachers in each of the two sites back to their classrooms and observed their teaching and then interviewed them about it. There, we documented all six teachers using strategies that we had observed firsthand during the 5-week institute, such as establishing writing groups and instituting the "author's chair." These were just two among many strategies they employed to help students share their writing and benefit from peer critique. In addition, we saw the teachers spark writing ideas and motivate reading, in both all-English and bilingual classrooms, by adopting lessons they had seen demonstrated during the summer institutes. When we asked the six about their instructional approaches, they gave explicit credit to what they had learned at the summer institute or subsequent continuity sessions.

Second, we asked the six teachers to follow two to three students for a year, each of whom represented a particular challenge to their work. They tracked and documented these students' academic progress, detailing assignments and interventions along the way. The resultant narratives provided us a glimpse into how the teachers attempted to instantiate "the work" into their actual classroom practice. By the time we had completed our study, we left convinced that what these six teachers had learned through the NWP affected what they did in classrooms and, therefore, what their students experienced there.

Nevertheless, this sample of six teachers is quite small, particularly given a national network that supports 175 local sites. Our study, therefore, provides only an initial, small-scale look into how teachers put lessons they learn in the NWP to work in their class-rooms, tailoring them for particular contexts and students.

A bigger question is how widespread such successes actually are. A major problem of networks anywhere (and other forms of decentralized professional development) is the problem of quality control. In the NWP, the national office must strike a delicate bal-ance. While it attempts to ensure that each site follows the basic "teachers-at-the-center"(Gray, 2000) model, it must also supply ample room and support so that each site can respond to local teachers' concerns and contexts.

In striking that balance, the NWP has developed a number of strategies to meet a variety of challenges, including changing demographics, mushrooming growth, and waves of intensifying public pressure for school reform. Since the NWP receives federal funding, it is now required to provide an annual review of every site, including evaluations of all events, and, more recently, an extensive and growing web-based communication system.

In its typical fashion, the NWP has made of its annual review process a professional development opportunity, and it has done so on multiple levels. The reviews themselves consist of a lengthy written discussion of the total program, including both summer and schoolyear work. Each site director writes a comprehensive review of goals and a thorough description of the year's work. All events are weighed in terms of previously set goals, and these assessments give guidance for the setting of future plans. Read by a committee of TCs and directors, the annual reports illuminate who needs help and what lessons are being learned, including what strategies and formats seem particularly promising and need ongoing support. For the committee, the review of the annual reports serves more than an evaluation function for the network. It also builds community as it affords professional development for those in leadership.

Another strategy to ensure high-quality teaching is to organize small networks of sites for sharing effective practices. Initially the NWP organized regional networks, clustering sites across con-tiguous states and appointing a regional coordinator. Early regional networks proved effective in areas of the South, the Mid-Atlantic, and the West, sometimes overlapping with state networks. However, by the mid-1980s local sites had identified a need to create special focus networks more closely tied to specific challenges of context or practice. The first of these was the Urban Sites Network, a network of local sites interested in the particular problems of urban teaching and the need for representation of racial and ethnic minorities in leadership. As an organized network, the Urban Sites Network mounted a substantial program of action research and site development, involving the work of teachers from 11 cities. These teachers work together to develop new knowledge regarding effective strategies for teaching writing in urban schools and then disseminate it throughout the network.

As they began to make progress on urban issues, the NWP sponsored another initiative—*Project Outreach*, a site development network focused on improving the quality of NWP services to teachers in low-income areas, both rural and urban. Lessons learned from Project Outreach, then, led to further investment in networks focusing on rural areas, on teaching English-language learners, and on creating sustained teacher-research communities. In uncovering ongoing region-specific problems, the national office stays close to actual problems teachers experience in their classrooms. In turn, site directors, by networking at the national level, perceive the range and persistence of systemic problems and then find ways to network high-quality, informed responses to local challenges.

The NWP recognizes that ensuring quality in the midst of growth is essential to the network's mission. Because of this, the national office has put one of the site directors in charge of an extensive program to provide assistance to regional sites that need it, including those in the first stages of formation. This person now works full-time for the NWP providing assistance to site directors. Because the NWP now receives extensive federal funding, she must also support any sites in danger of not meeting federal requirements. Also in the spirit of ensuring the quality and success of new sites, each site director is now supported by a mentor who is an experienced site director. Thus, new directors learn from the hard-won success of seasoned veterans.

Internal strategies, such as those described above, are now being bolstered by external supports. As mentioned in Chapter 1, in 1999 the Academy for Educational Development (AED) began conducting a 3-year national evaluation of the NWP. The goal of the evaluation was to collect data on how NWP teachers develop student writing in their classrooms, the specific conditions that support student achievement in writing, and what outcomes for students are being produced in NWP classrooms. During the first year AED collected teacher assignments and students' work. The study, involving nearly 600 third- and fourth-grade students and 24 teachers from Writing Project sites throughout the United States, found the following:

- Teachers described many ways in which the Writing Project changed their philosophy about teaching and teaching practices.
- Most NWP teachers took on leadership roles in their school, district, or state by providing professional development to their colleagues.
- NWP teachers spend much more time on writing instruction than do most fourth-grade teachers across the country.
- NWP teachers give writing assignments that are diverse and represent a wide range of types of assignments.
- A majority of teacher assignments provided students with an opportunity to perform authentic intellectual work.
- Students' work also showed evidence of construction of knowledge.
- The study confirmed the finding of Newmann and Wehlage (1995) that students were more likely to construct knowledge when the assignment they were responding to made an explicit call to do so (Fancsali, Nelsestuen, & Weinbaum, 2001a)

During year 2, AED (Fancsali, Nelsestuen, & Weinbaum, 2001) did an analysis of teacher assignments as well as conducting written surveys and telephone interviews with 29 Writing Project teachers from five sites across the country. It also administered writing "prompts" and received writing samples from more than 700 third- and fourth-graders. The data revealed, as in year 1, that the NWP had a profound impact on the participating third- and fourth-grade teachers' beliefs and practices. And it showed the many ways in which participating teachers foster student achievement in writing and use writing as a tool for learning.

Inverness Research Associates (St. John et al., 2001) has done a large-scale survey assessing NWP participants' satisfaction with their professional development experiences as well as the impact of professional development programs on participants' subsequent classroom practices. They found that teachers who participated in NWP invitational institutes reported a year later that they had gained valuable knowledge and skills from the institute and had changed their classroom practices as a result. In very high proportions, teachers claimed numerous benefits from the summer institutes. Of the teachers responding, 95% reported gaining concrete teaching strategies; 93% said the institute brought them up to date on the latest research and practice; 91% said that they are now motivated to seek more professional development; and 88% said they had found specific ways to assess student work and plan teaching. Eighty-six percent said they are better able to teach more diverse students, while 85% said they are better able to help students reach standards. A high proportion of teachers surveyed reported they believed their students had benefited from the changes (St. John, et al., 2001).

However, the tension between what participants learn in a network and what they do with that learning is still a critical problem. Although during our study we witnessed firsthand teachers using strategies and organizing learning activities in ways they had learned from their summer institutes, clearly a larger study needs to be done with many more teachers in different sites. Although we completed our study convinced that six teachers—and many of the others we interviewed—have enlarged their professional repertoires and honed their ability to match teaching strategies to individual children's needs, there is still much to learn about many more teachers. How, on a much larger scale, does the NWP "way of learning" make a difference to teachers and to their students? How many sites work as well as the two we studied? The NWP, however, is engaged in an ongoing effort to pursue these questions on a number of fronts and with a number of partners while it subjects its own practices to continuous examination and improvement.

NETWORKS EMBEDDED IN SCHOOL–UNIVERSITY PARTNERSHIPS

The NWP, like a number of other reform efforts, depends on a school–university partnership arrangement. This relationship makes the NWP a special kind of reform because it joins the knowledge of the university with the knowledge developed by teachers. In theory, many people now accept the fact that teachers develop knowledge as they teach students over the years, and some believe it to be of critical importance. Nevertheless, the university has traditionally privileged theoretical knowledge over practitioner knowledge. Creating a partnership where these two forms of knowledge can intersect and build on each other demands rethinking the nature of knowledge from a more egalitarian perspective. It also demands new approaches to governance within the partnership. Universities engaged in such partnerships must make room for a "third space," one housed in the university, while retaining a measure of independence from the regular program of studies. One such arrangement exists at the UCLA site, where the NWP, though part of the pre-service program, also operates as an independent professional development program. Such a unique partnership could not exist without enlightened leadership involving an extended sense of mission from the university and the school of education.

Such partnerships can create a daunting array of challenges. Equitable relationships in school–university partnerships are frequently elusive, despite university lip service to working with "the field." In many cases, the university controls the agenda and the resources, rendering practitioners subservient to university interests (Lieberman, 1992). In the case of NWP partnerships with universities, such a hierarchical relationship could be especially devastating since it contradicts its fundamental mission, that is, making teacher knowledge rather than university research knowledge the *starting* place for improvement.

Each NWP partnership has its own local history, of course, but as a general rule, writing or composition has low status as an academic area in the university. That propensity, coupled with the problems and time it takes to "work with the field," contributes to the fragility of NWP school–university partnerships. University professors and instructors are seldom officially rewarded for working with practitioners, even though for the last few decades this continues to be a recommended practice for the sake of school reform. Despite the fact that a number of the directors have become recognized regional or national educational leaders, some continue to hold marginal positions in the university. Such difficulties demand that site leaders become adept at brokering resources, people, and programs as they navigate between the culture of the university and the culture of the NWP sites.

At UCLA, for instance, leadership has been very stable. There are two co-directors, one who has been inside the university as an instructor since 1977 and the other who was a teacher and a very popular and knowledgeable staff developer in her own district before she came to UCLA. The directors have learned how to make the strengths of the NWP model visible. As explained in Chapter 3, after years of being housed outside the school of education (but within the university), the site is now a part of a center established to work with schools. Because of strong leadership, sponsorship by a high-status professor, and years of serving teachers in Los Angeles, the site has gained a strong and well-deserved reputation, which has given it, in turn, unusual legitimacy within the university.

By situating NWP sites in college settings, despite all these challenges, the network has acquired the status necessary to sustain its work for nearly three decades in locations all over the country.

Partnering with universities, despite the attendant challenges, has been one of the NWP's greatest strengths and accomplishments. Born as a partnership between university-based and school-based teachers, the NWP consistently finds ways to have K–university teachers working together in the struggle to produce more literate citizens.

NETWORKS, PARTNERSHIPS, AND COALITIONS: OCCUPYING A "THIRD SPACE"

In the 1990s a number of studies of networks and partnerships sought to explain how they operate, what makes teachers belong to them, what contributions they make, and what challenges they face (Cochran-Smith & Lytle, 1999; Cuban, 1992; Lieberman & Grolnick, 1996; Westheimer, 1998; Wineburg & Grossman, 1998). Elyse Aidman-Aadahl, as we explained in Chapter 2, described the NWP as occupying a "third space." We concur. Confined neither within universities nor within schools, the NWP brings people, strengths, and concerns from both universities and schools together. While attentive to the local realities and governance of the institutions it seeks to influence, the network retains a measure of autonomy outside them. In doing so, the NWP creates a web of relationships that provide opportunities for people to collaborate both formally, through professional development opportunities, and informally, through interpersonal contacts. While networking educators nationally and regionally, the NWP invites them to bring to the table local concerns and problems for collective dialogue and inquiry. Thus, it foregrounds the everyday, real concerns of educators against a larger horizon of educational issues, and then helps to build knowledge and expertise and distribute them where they are needed. The "third space" of the NWP, then, is both local and remote, grounded in and yet transcendent of particular institutions, and facilitative of both formal professional development experiences and informal personal connections.

These fluid organizational characteristics make networks uniquely qualified to cross traditional boundaries in order to accommodate contemporary conditions of rapid change (Lieberman & Grolnick, 1996). Linking school knowledge and university knowledge, they tend to be collaborative rather than hierarchical, and they find ways for "inside knowledge" (the knowledge that teachers create on the job) to inform "outside knowledge" (the knowledge of reformers, researchers, and policy makers), and vice versa. Moreover, networks like the NWP bridge the traditional boundaries that separate teachers, keeping them from collaborating with one another. These boundaries include those around subject-area departments, grade levels, socioeconomic backgrounds of students, and so forth (McLaughlin & Talbert, 2001).

Flexibility is a key characteristic of networks. The NWP, for instance, rather than promoting a "best approach," encourages teachers to develop numerous strategies in order to respond to particular students' needs. Teachers feel free to tap into a variety of sources of outside knowledge, while creating innovative formats to develop and consume knowledge built from practice. The network extends leadership opportunities to teachers that they might not otherwise experience, and it creates collaborative working relationships among schools, universities, districts, and state and federal departments of education.

Despite creating these permeable boundaries with other institutions, the NWP manages to impart to its members a strong sense of network identity without weakening teachers' ties to primary institutions. In the two sites we studied, teachers claimed that the NWP had given them a new sense of themselves and their professional responsibilities to their students, their school, and the teaching profession. They felt compelled to share their best work, read research and other literature, explore and discuss ideas pertaining to literacy, inquire into their own practice, and take on leadership roles. Successful networks tend to instill such cultural norms for professionalism even as they work with other organizations whose norms may be quite different. How NWP sites manage to do this is a complex undertaking, given the historical, political, economic, and social contexts of institutions and the individual personnel inhabiting them. Coming to understand this better deserves a study in itself.

Creating, occupying, and sustaining a "third space" is always difficult. Network leadership must continuously negotiate the changing political landscape and find ways to maintain autonomy. Besides navigating the power relations involving universities, our two sites, 20 years old and 7 years old, had to deal with state policies pressing them to succumb to a narrower and more prescriptive view of literacy and school improvement. At UCLA, the teachers struggled to figure out how to find a way to deal with a mandated reading curriculum, while at OSU they coped with an intensifying use of standardized tests to measure student achievement and school quality. Finding ways to support teachers in policy contexts that narrow curricular choices is increasingly a problem for NWP sites.

MODELS AND PRACTICES, NOT PRESCRIPTIONS AND RECIPES

Networks flourish to the extent that they attract participants around compelling ideas without producing a constraining orthodoxy. In other words, a healthy network must win commitment to particular principles or ideals while also providing opportunities for intellectual challenge and new membership. The NWP is just such a network. Its model for professional development consistently applies the principles that teachers' knowledge is valuable and that it needs to be surfaced and made public. It insists that teachers have something to teach other teachers. Along with those principles, the NWP has made a strong commitment to the notions of writing-as-process and writing-to-learn.

The network, however, cannot afford to ignore outside perceptions that misconstrue its work. Some outsiders have mistakenly conflated the NWP approach with a prescription for step-by-step writing workshops. Others have confused the NWP's emphasis on student choice and authentic authorship with "anything goes." Still others have claimed that when "teachers teach other teachers," they insulate themselves from needed outside expertise. As a result, there have been charges that the NWP concerns itself more with processes than with intellectual substance.

These critics, however, fail to recognize how carefully the NWP wards off this danger by building certain intellectual safeguards into the structure of its summer institutes and all other subsequent professional development initiatives. During the summer, fellows encounter a curriculum shaped not only by the expertise of colleagues but also by current knowledge in the field of literacy. Although all fellows engage in writing and belong to writing response groups, they do not follow rigid, sequential processes. Rather, they compose in their own ways, on their own topics, and in their own styles and make their approaches transparent in their writing groups. In addition, during the teaching demonstrations, they see firsthand multiple ways to approach writing and writing instruction. For instance, during the summer institutes we saw various approaches to generating topics, including brainstorming and building concept maps. Some suggested viewing a film or hearing a compelling story as inspiration. Others recommended autobiographical writing or engaging in warm-up exercises such as free writing or peer dialogue. During the institutes, fellows discuss the particular demands of writing in different genres and of attending to different audiences. They read about, experiment with, and discuss theories of rhetoric and convention as well as attendant implications for writing instruction.

Ultimately, sentimental and simplistic approaches to writing instruction simply cannot stand up to the critical dialogue and scholarly research, which are always a part of NWP gatherings. Moreover, as the NWP increasingly invites the scrutiny of diverse perspectives, it pushes for deeper questions and more complex understandings regarding literacy. For instance, the NWP has worked particularly hard—with notable success—to bring into its ranks teachers of color (Fancsali, et al., 2001), who frequently raise challenging issues about dominant discourses and conventions. It has also invited the perspectives of teachers and students from rural schools. And it welcomes the introduction of hot-button controversies into professional development conversations, such as those surrounding standardized tests, bilingual education, and the teaching of reading. As it seeks to make room for increasing intellectual diversity, the NWP attempts to shield itself from intellectual sloppiness.

As with any reform network that attempts to change teacher practice, however, the NWP's survival depends, in part, on its rep-

utation. The problem becomes how to make the mission suffi-
ciently accessible to attract potential funders and new members
without oversimplifying it. We learned how difficult this task is,
especially in the present policy context, where talk of accountability pervades public debates on education. Ironically, the NWP's
continued success has much to do with the ways in which it has
organized and put into practice a set of interrelated social and
intellectual practices (described in Chapter 2) that ultimately place
substantial professional responsibility on the shoulders of teachers
to collectively develop effective ways to reach changing student
populations in changing times. In accomplishing this, the NWP
has avoided the reading and writing ideological wars that have
alienated many teachers. But the problem remains of how to convey such a complex approach when the public, politicians, and
policy makers continue to lean toward quick fixes that produce
packages, programs, and sound bites.

VOLUNTEERISM VERSUS CONSCRIPTION

For many years, change theorists have been debating whether
change comes about through mandate or volunteerism. In the
NWP, teachers apply to come to a summer institute, and there is a
review process for their selection. One charge made against the
NWP is that it serves those already motivated to improve and, as
those who favor mandates claim, does not reach teachers who
really need to improve. This rationale often serves as justification
for mandated and prescribed improvement programs for teachers,
even though the evidence shows that these programs have had
weak results over time (Cohen, 1990; Darling-Hammond, 1990;
McLaughlin & Talbert, 2001).

The NWP claims that respect for teacher knowledge during the
summer institutes not only releases that knowledge but also moti-
vates participants to continue to improve after the institutes.
Teachers with these sensibilities, then, become the TCs who turn
around and conduct professional development experiences for
their peers. Such an approach promotes the articulation of tacit

knowledge and the collegial exchange of ideas and skills, setting the conditions for ongoing professional learning. Does this mean that professional development "the NWP way" is powerful enough to affect large numbers of teachers no matter what length of time they are involved or what kinds of organized activities they participate in? These questions deserve further study.

Perhaps the NWP approach suggests another way of looking at the volunteerism–conscription dichotomy. Perhaps that dichotomy has obscured larger questions about motivating teachers to learn and grow. What the NWP seems to understand is that what *teachers know* should be the starting place for professional development. Working from that premise has made NWP professional development experiences particularly compelling for teachers.

Another issue has to do with who sets the agenda for professional development. In Oklahoma, for example, we saw the OSU site working within the constraints of a mandated curriculum in at least one district. Because TCs in the OSU site have developed a reputation for engaging teachers in their own improvement, they are often called upon to help implement such mandates. At the UCLA site, TCs worked with teachers to implement a reading program, again one that had been mandated in the district. In each case, TCs went willingly but on their own terms: voluntary participation, multiple sessions, and respect for teacher knowledge and experience. In each case, TCs struggled to help colleagues fulfill mandates without surrendering larger aims for students' learning, such as ownership, voice, dialogue, and critical thinking. According to TCs, the point is to construct the problem of mandates not as an exercise in compliance but as an opportunity for creativity. Teachers, they believe, can work together to organize learning activities so that they serve multiple objectives without sacrificing coherence and meaning.

These were cases of teachers deeply engaged in professional learning because they had extended opportunities to recognize and articulate what they know (and what they don't know) as they struggle to meet outside demands, especially those they see as contrary to their own intentions. Instead of getting stymied in the volunteerism-versus-conscription debate, perhaps the NWP's approach to involving teachers in their own improvement suggests a path that would make the debate no longer necessary. By motivating large numbers of teachers to continuous improvement and building the capacity of teachers to lead others to do so in their schools, the NWP has shown repeatedly that, when treated respectfully and offered opportunities to reach students, teachers seem to respond energetically. Perhaps the NWP approach suggests a model for professional development writ large—regardless of the subject matter. Many have questioned whether any other subject matter can engage teachers the way writing can, but there have been other subject-matter networks that have organized their members on similar grounds with similar results (Little, 1993).

THE CHANGING SOCIAL AND POLITICAL CONTEXT

As this book is being written, the social and political contexts for schooling are becoming increasingly rigid and test-driven. Models of student choice, greater student involvement in the learning process, and varieties of group strategies are giving way to prescribed curricula, scripts for teachers, and accountability measured solely by test scores. The NWP contributes a powerful alternative to the latter, however. In inviting teachers to be both knowers and learners, it creates forums for them to share what they learn from practice, to be conscious of how they learn, to practice becoming writers and readers, and to be intellectuals and professionals. But how can the NWP maintain this stance in light of the prescriptive models that are increasingly becoming *the* curriculum mandated by many districts? How will the NWP teachers sustain their excitement for the learning process even as many teachers are feeling constrained by mandated programs and increased external testing?

This question dogged us during our study, but we found that NWP teachers talked about outside mandates in surprising ways. Instead of resorting to a knee-jerk rejection of these sorts of mandates, TCs tend to discuss them with one another and to look for potential value in them. If they can discern little value, they try to find ways just to live with them. When possible, they organize student learning in order to implement the mandates while also satisfying their own educational aims for students. The stance they tend to take is to *engage* rather than *rebel*.

Nevertheless, TCs complained repeatedly that current educational policies dismissed their knowledge and professional judgment. Too many reforms are proposed and enacted by policy makers who don't fully grasp the implications for classroom teaching and learning (Check, 2000). Although the NWP is sometimes in philosophical disagreement with school reforms, its existence enables teachers to adapt and modify these initiatives so that they actually work in their classrooms. Nevertheless, while teachers learn early on that reform ideas come and go, prolonged pressure to conform takes a toll. Negotiation between outside mandates and teacher efficacy will be a continuing challenge for the NWP.

MANAGING COMPLEXITY, DIVERSITY, AND CHANGE AS A NETWORK

The health of the NWP as a network depends on its ability to recognize its problems wherever and whenever they arise and to use those problems as a springboard for further learning and improvement. The NWP's success in building ongoing learning communities, as the change literature describes (Fullan & Hargreaves, 1996; McLaughlin & Talbert, 2001), accounts for its continuing viability and the commitment of participants. Nevertheless, maintaining ever-expanding learning communities involves management of complexity, and it keeps the NWP in a state of constant dynamic tension. The national leadership must remain vigilant, looking for what and where the needs are and then troubleshooting continuously as the political contexts change and new interests and problems emerge. Similarly, the national office must support fledgling sites, those that have been in existence for a while, and everything in between. And all of this must be done with an eye to changing conditions in this country and the larger world that place demands on teachers, schools, and universities. Perhaps both a reason for and an indication of its success is that the NWP has had great stability in its top leadership, having had only two directors since its founding in 1974. This is a remarkable record in a network of such complexity.

Successful networks do not fear reinventing themselves from time to time, looking critically at their mission, how it is being served, and whether it needs to be expanded to meet new needs (Lieberman & Grolnick, 1996). Managing change while keeping the network organization stable creates a tension that is of greater importance to networks than formal organizations because they must maintain their legitimacy to members even as they modify or alter their positions and activities to meet the changing social and political conditions. Creating special-interest networks (Urban Sites, Rural Sites, English Language Learners, Teacher Inquiry Communities) and projects that bring sites together to work on particular problems (such as the Focus on Standards project) has been one way the NWP has dealt with these tensions. Managing the growing complexity of the network, particularly given current social and political changes, will further test its adaptability and viability. So far, the mission of the NWP has inspired many teachers and motivated them to become active TCs. But a continuing challenge for the NWP will be to establish a compelling vision that continues to attract teachers, while also responding to shifting times, local demands, and growing numbers of new members. This is a problem, endemic to all networks, that simply will not go away.

Local Site Leadership

The mission of the NWP is to inspire and motivate teachers to participate in professional development for themselves and their peers, and it is in a larger sense an important step toward the professionalization of teaching. The work of accomplishing this mission is rooted in the particular context of each local site, which must adapt the vision and the practices to local problems and challenges. Since the director of a site is a nexus of the social and political context of the schools and districts, he or she must bridge the inevitable misunderstandings and conflicts, making it possible for people from different cultures to communicate with, learn from, and support one another.

A site director must know not only how to mount a 5-week invitational but how to attend to the needs of teachers and the organization itself. It is important to stay abreast of major educational issues of the day, interpreting them and incorporating them into the work of professional development. As we observed at the sites we studied, the success of their programs depended in large measure on the skillful brokering of relationships within their university as well as the district and state. Both sites had established traditions of stable leadership, and the current directors managed the complexities with great skill.

Having studied only two directors, both quite successful, we still do not know enough about how other directors lead and negotiate these complex roles. How do they acquire the necessary skills and abilities? Indeed, what qualities does a director need to do the job well? What do directors bring to the position, and what do they learn on the job? What might be codified and learned, and what must be intuitive and improvisational? If the site is as leadership-dependent as it appears to be, then much more work has to be done to understand what directors do as they develop a site in their particular contexts and how they deal with the problems that inevitably arise.

Aware of the importance of supporting and learning from the site directors, the NWP has held an annual 4-day retreat for site directors and co-directors over the past 5 years. Approximately 30 site leaders have attended each year. In addition, the NWP offers technical assistance to sites that need help, providing learning opportunities for directors. Learning more about how directors learn and how to support these leaders in this period of rapid educational change seems necessary for the continued growth and health of the network.

Teacher Consultants

As couriers of the NWP's values, the TCs are at the heart of its work. They reach out to one another and to teachers outside the network in pursuit of better ways to teach and reach students. The strength of this model lies in the ongoing opportunities for TCs to be leaders as well as learners. The danger is burn-out, since there is no end to the amount of work available for a TC in a successful site. It was apparent at both UCLA and OSU that active TCs carry an extraordinarily heavy load. The six teachers we studied worked hard in their own schools to meet difficult local challenges while also shouldering numerous responsibilities as TCs. Their accomplishments and their problems reflect what we perceive as a tension inherent in the NWP model.

The fundamental infrastructure of the NWP is the growing cadre of experienced teachers prepared to teach other teachers. These teachers work as TCs, as classroom teachers, and as NWP colleagues, and in many cases they have family responsibilities as well. Obviously, these responsibilities make for a heavy load for anyone to carry. Four of the experienced TCs we studied were deeply involved in NWP work, and the two initiates were poised to do the same. The active TCs served on curriculum committees, gave teaching demonstrations, took college courses, served on advisory boards, played leadership roles in their local sites and districts, contributed to newsletters and online discussions, and attended continuity workshops. They were also classroom teachers.

Although we realize that we cannot generalize from the TCs in this small sample, we suspect from talking to site and national directors that the load that they carry is not atypical. It is important for the NWP to find ways to deal with the potential overload on TCs. For example, it may want to find ways to encourage more TCs to play an active role, particularly in sites where there are large teacher populations. It may want to continue to find different kinds of professional arrangements for TCs. For example, a TC at the UCLA site works half time teaching high school English and half time for the NWP. Perhaps more opportunities should be created for 1-year leaves and time during the schoolday for planning and implementing professional development.

We wondered if there might be other ways, some already practiced and some possible, to think about the work of TCs. TCs are not the only teachers who have become invisible partners and leaders for the sake of improving schools. When teachers take on additional responsibilities for other teachers' learning, they continue to enhance their own understandings of teaching and learning, but they also increase their professional burdens. Continual efforts need to be made to institutionalize leadership roles for TCs in order to protect them from overload and burn-out.

A Model for Professional Development

Our study helped us to understand why some teachers said that the NWP "transformed" their lives. Through observations of the institutes, interviews with TCs in both sites, and in-depth observations of and discussions with the six teachers, we found that the NWP amounts to much more than inspiration. It strongly influences how teachers think about their own professional roles, changes what they do in classrooms, and affects how and what students learn.

The NWP form of professional development contradicts traditional practice, which is typically based on presentations and workshops led by academics and staff developers. It begins with knowledge that teachers have accrued over the years and provides a format that makes it possible for teachers to present that knowledge to one another and construct new knowledge while also engaging theoretical knowledge.

Instead of teachers passively listening to a speaker, who most often presents decontextualized, generic knowledge and skills, teachers become active participants in learning as they discover together new approaches to teaching literacy and then apply them in their classrooms. Instead of having to choose between theoretical and practical knowledge, they learn ways to connect the two. Instead of taking classes in leadership at the local university, NWP teachers have opportunities to actually develop leadership skills as they contribute to the professional development of other teachers. Instead of thinking of leadership as something a principal does, teachers are encouraged to facilitate learning for their peers, create and lead work groups, do research, share and discuss articles and books, read and write for publication, and so forth. Instead of presenting teachers with language arts content standards as if they were a list of "shoulds," teachers show each other specifically how to align their practices with standards.

Instead of assuming that all teachers are the same regardless of age, experience, and context, the NWP approach allows for their differences. Instead of a one-shot professional development workshop, the NWP creates follow-up sessions and ongoing relationships to support learning. Instead of feeling isolated and disengaged from professional development, teachers encounter a searching, inquiring community that promises to support better teaching practices and that drives home the idea that good teaching requires continuous learning. Instead of thinking about teaching as a solo effort, Writing Project teachers have opportunities to engage with others in continually shaping a network that is rooted in teachers' questions, that adapts to changing conditions, and that models professional work as a collective as well as an individual effort.

These practices create "increasing levels of participation within a community as well as the changing modes of participation" (Lave & Wenger, 1991, p. 53) and give teachers opportunities to improve. The social practices embedded in NWP professional development not only build community but also encourage intellectual development. What might seem simple at first glance turns out to be a complex intertwining of process and content, the personal and the professional, the individual and the collective, the intellectual and the social, the short term and the long haul. Future research will be needed to untangle these threads in order to understand the workings of the NWP as an organization and as a model for professional development.

PROFESSIONAL DEVELOPMENT: JOINING INQUIRY AND COMMUNITY IN A NETWORK CONTEXT

On the face of it, the NWP strategy appears to be directed toward changing teachers one at a time, a strategy that would have limited impact on the teaching of writing and on the profession as a whole. This characterization masks a far more complex strategy, involving strategies of change and professional development both for individuals and for communities within a network context.

Teachers come to the invitational as individuals, but most go home as members of a community. They fulfill their responsibilities as community members by becoming TCs and facilitating professional development for others in their profession, creating new ties and relationships. Rather than a strategy for changing teachers one by one, the NWP has launched a far more complex undertaking involving both individual and collective learning. Processes that release their own accumulated knowledge and grant them exposure to the knowledge of colleagues whets the appetites of teachers for further learning. Professional dialogue and scholarship become an ongoing commitment, and these, in turn, build and disseminate knowledge in ways that influence classroom practices.

Despite the revitalization and renewal teachers gain from the NWP experiences, they still must go back to their schools and negotiate their own school cultures. In our sample, the two new teachers, who had just been to the invitational the year we began the study, went back to their schools and made concrete efforts to reach out to colleagues, promote collective professional learning, and effect needed changes for students. One created a new form of professional development in her school, which resulted in the formation of a "writing group." The other increased her influence in her district by providing evidence that she could raise her students' test scores while teaching the NWP way. Both teachers, from schools with large bilingual populations, were inspired to create change. In several cases, we saw schools where there were enough NWP teachers to form powerful alliances and professional communities. In one, for instance, five teachers, the vice principal, and the principal had attended past invitationals and worked together to influence the school culture and teaching practices. A study involving a much larger sample of teacher consultants might illuminate how many TCs are able to make similar contributions and under what institutional conditions.

Thus, focusing on one level of analysis—the individual teacher—can give us only a part of the whole story. Individuals are part of that whole, but they cannot be properly understood outside of their professional development contexts: the NWP network, the site network, their schools and classrooms. Only by looking carefully at all these levels did we come to understand the "multiple embedded contexts" that influenced teachers' lives in the NWP (McLaughlin & Talbert, 2001, p. 146).

In observing experienced TCs, who provided a window for viewing what teaching as a profession has the potential to become, we saw how network relationships could inspire teachers to become leaders in the continual quest for school reform. Networks such as the NWP can create new models for professional development rooted in teachers' individual and collective learning—professional development that is not only instruction in a particular subject or program but also an essential and career-long responsibility.

The NWP professional community provides a powerful context for professional learning and continuous collective inquiry (Cochran-Smith & Lytle, 1993; Darling-Hammond, 1997; Elmore & Burney, 1999; McLaughlin & Talbert, 2001; Sykes, 1999). By moving between the institute, the network, and individual teachers, we have begun to understand the complexity of this community and the web of knowledge and relationships that makes it grow and change. This study is only a first step in understanding the links between what teachers learn in their networks, what they do in their classrooms, and how this affects their students' achievement and accomplishment.

Research Design: Teacher Development in a Network Context

Because of the emerging evidence that networks provide a powerful context for teacher development, we sought to understand from the "inside" how the National Writing Project—arguably the most successful professional development program in the United States—provides this kind of development. We met in the winter of 1997 to get the support of the directors of the NWP. We agreed that in our study we would (1) connect the project as much as possible to the link between teacher and student learning, (2) attend to the role of practitioners in the creation, management, and sustenance of teacher networks, and (3) raise and amplify teachers' voices on their own terms and from their own perspectives.

The Research Questions

We asked the following questions:

1. How do these two different sites enable (or constrain) teacher development and student learning in the classroom?
2. What are the key attributes of these sites, and how do they provide for technical learning and the building of a professional community?
3. What strategies are developed to address (and respond to) the particulars of the network contexts both locally and nationally?

Site and Teacher Selection

Our criteria for the selection of sites was: an urban and a rural site and differences in geography, years of operation, size, and cultural context. We sought the recommendations of the directors at the national NWP office, who suggested the sites at UCLA and OSU. Our idea was for each of us to concentrate deeply on one site. Since Ann Lieberman grew up in Los Angeles and went to UCLA, she went to that site, while Diane Wood went to OSU.

With the help of the UCLA and OSU directors, we chose three teachers from each site, one fairly new teacher and new to the NWP, a TC who had taught for more than 5 years, and a veteran TC. In this way we reasoned that we could get a better sense of whether the learnings from the invitational lasted and could be observed in classrooms.

Research Methods

During our 2-year study we collected multiple sources of data in a variety of ways, including site visits with face-to-face interviews, collection of WP documents, and e-mail correspondence.

- *Site visits* to both sites for 2 years—three to four times to each site each year.
- *Documentation* of the 5-week summer institute in both sites and a sampling of all the other offerings at both sites, including teacher-researcher groups and workshops on How to Organize Workshops, Preparing for the National Board for Professional Teaching Standards, Teaching Writing to English Language Learners, The Socratic Method, Writing Camps for Students, Assessing Student's Writing and Reading Ability, and Project Outreach (at OSU). Each of these professional development offerings were observed by us and four NWP TCs who attended, observed, and described these sessions.
- *Interviews* with national leadership, site directors, target teachers, and other teachers at each site and following up by email. The number of interviews varied, but we held at

least three intensive interviews with the six targeted
teachers.

- *Classroom observations* (three times at each site) of six teachers. We also interviewed them on site. The classroom observations and lengthy interviews took half a day. We then followed up on their classroom work by email. All teachers
  collected student work to show the growth of students over
  a year's time.
- *Focus group* discussions with teacher consultants were conducted at least twice at each site and with all six teachers
  and their site directors together at UCLA.
- *Narratives* written by the six teachers about two to three of
  their students, including assessments of student work collected over time to show student progress. Our intent was
  to have teachers write narratives of three students that
  were of interest to them, such as students who were especially problematic or interesting or who played particular
  roles in the classroom. Diane Wood taught teachers at both
  sites how to use narratives as data at a full-day session at
  UCLA. The target teachers and other interested teachers
  were invited. A similar workshop day was held at OSU.
  These workshops were intended to provide opportunities
  for teachers to learn to use narratives as data to be used in
  better understanding their teaching and learning intentions with particular students and to show how their
  Writing Project understanding is displayed in their everyday work.

Both the 1-day workshop and the subsequent writing of the
teachers became a professional development effort far beyond
anything that we had expected. The teachers focused heavily on
their teaching and its impact on their students and reported learning a great deal about what they were (and weren't) doing with
their students. We include the workshop format below for anyone
who is interested in using narratives as data, as a professional
development effort, or as a means for discussion of learning about
the connections between teacher intent and impact on students.

TEACHING STORIES AS QUALITATIVE DATA

8:30–9:00 Introductions

9:00–9:45 Teaching Stories as Data: How and Why?

Narrative language as interruption and disruption
Stories as carriers of the specific, the local, the idiosyncratic
Teaching stories as departure points for systematic inquiry
But isn't this all too subjective?
— Or what's omitted, biased, or self-interested here?
Teaching stories and professional ethics
Collaborative storytelling: There's strength—and validity—in
    numbers

10:00–11:00 Narrating Teaching Experiences

Please write:

One tale of woe, or "Why did I get myself into this
impossible profession?" (This story should chronicle a time
when you believe you failed to provide a meaningful learning experience for a particular student or class.)
    One tale of success, or "Hello!—I'm really good at this."
(This story should be an account of providing a powerful
learning experience for a student or class.)

11:00–12:00 Collaborative Storytelling

During this hour, you are going to concentrate on the tales of
woe. Please give time for each person to read his or her story and
then consider both stories in light of the following questions.

1. What do your stories "say" about continuing problems,
   challenges, and dilemmas in teaching? What do they fail to
   say? Could the stories be "fleshed out" with more convincing details or explanations without losing the narrative
   power? If so, how?

2. What might policy makers, parents, administrators, district officials, or other outside audiences learn from these stories?
3. As you look at the conflict or the problem in your stories, how might your learning from or participation in the Writing Project serve as an aid to finding paths toward resolution, solution, or transformation?
4. What might not be believed or taken seriously by outside audiences? Why? Whose perspective might you have omitted or ignored? How might your story be critiqued? How might you strengthen your story against those who might doubt or refute you?
5. How might your "tales of woe" serve as interruptions or disruptions to business-as-usual in public schools locally or nationally?
6. When you look at these "tales of woe" separately and together, what insights do you have about conditions and approaches that foster student learning? How might you collect/create evidence that would support the right conditions and approaches, as you define them?

1:00–2:00 Repeat Collaborative Storytelling Process

Stay with your partner. Repeat the process above with the tales of success, using these questions:

1. What do your stories "say" about the conditions and approaches that successfully promote student learning? What do they fail to say? Could the stories be "fleshed out" with more convincing details or explanations without losing the narrative power? If so, how?
2. What might policy makers, parents, administrators, district officials, or other outside audiences learn from these success stories?
3. As you look at the "crowing moment of success" in your story, how might this success serve as an example of the NWP principles or approaches? How might this successful moment be related to your participation in the Writing Project?

4. What might not be believed or taken seriously by outside audiences? Why? How might you strengthen your story against nay-sayers?
5. How might your "tales of success" serve as interruptions or disruptions to business-as-usual in public schools locally and nationally?
6. When you look at these "tales of success" separately and together, what insights do you have about conditions and approaches that foster student learning? How do these conditions and approaches relate to participation in the WP? How might you collect/create persuasive evidence that these conditions and approaches should pervade public schools?

2:00–2:45 Debriefing

Why share stories?
What can be learned from holding the stories in dialogue?
What is the role of reflection?
How can stories be "backed up" with additional evidence?
–Student work as evidence
–Interviewing
–Videotaping
–Field notes

3:00–4:00 Stories That Have Mattered and Looking Toward the Future

Data Analysis

We used a holistic approach to our data analysis, repeatedly reading through our interview transcripts, field notes, the TC's narratives, and NWP documents with our questions in mind. As themes and patterns emerged, we wrote them in the margins and frequently sought confirmation from research participants. Over time, it became clear to us that three big themes would form the basis of our story: the NWP as a growing and enduring network, the NWP as a unique culture, and the NWP as an influence on classroom practices. These themes eventually became the organizing framework for clustering our data.

References

Atwell, N. (1987). *In the middle: Writing, reading, and learning with adolescents.* Portsmouth, NH: Heinemann.

Atwell-Vasey, N. (1998). *Nourishing words: Bridging private reading and public teaching.* Albany: State University of New York Press.

Calkins, L. M. (1994). *The art of teaching writing* (Rev. ed.). Portsmouth, NH: Heinemann.

Check, J. (2000, September–October). Mandated reform vs. classroom reality. *The Voice,* pp. 4–5.

Cohen, D. K. (1990). Revolution in one classroom: The case of Mrs. Oublier. *Educational Evaluation and Policy Analysis, 12*(3), 311–330.

Cohn, M. M., & Kottkamp, R. B. (1993). *Teachers, the missing voice in education.* Albany: State University of New York Press.

Cochran-Smith, M., & Lytle, S. (1990). Research on teaching and teacher research: The issues that divide. *Educational Researcher, 19*(2), 2–11.

Cochran-Smith, M., & Lytle, S. (1993). *Inside/outside: Teacher research and knowledge.* New York: Teachers College Press.

Cochran-Smith, M., & Lytle, S. (1999). Teacher learning in professional communities: Three knowledge-practice relationships. In P. D. Pearson & A. Iran-Nejad (Eds.), *Review of Research in Education, 24,* 251–307.

Crandall, D. (1983). *People, policies and practices: Examining the chain of school improvement.* Andover, MA: The Network.

Cuban, L. (1992). Managing dilemmas while building professional communities. *Educational Researcher, 28*(7), 15–25.

Darling-Hammond, L. (1990). Instructional policy into practice: "The Power of the Bottom over the Top." *Educational Evaluation and Policy Analysis, 12*(3), 233–242.

Darling-Hammond, L. (1997). *The right to learn: A blueprint for creating schools that work.* San Francisco: Jossey-Bass.

Darling-Hammond, L. (1998). Policy and change: Getting beyond the bureaucracy. In A. Hargreaves, A. Lieberman, M. Fullan, & D.

Hopkins (Eds.), *The international handbook of educational change* (pp. 642–666). Dordrecht, The Netherlands: Kluwer.

Elbow, P. (1986). *Embracing contraries: Epiphanies in learning and teaching.* New York: Oxford University Press.

Elmore, R. F., & Burney, D. (1999). *Investing in teacher learning: Staff development and instructional improvement.* San Francisco: Jossey-Bass.

Fancsali, C., & Nelsestuen, K. (2001, November). *Evaluation of the National Writing Project, Overview of Year-two results* [Presentation to the NWP task force]. New York: Academy for Educational Development.

Fancsali, C., Nelsestuen, K., & Weinbaum, A. (2001a). *National Writing Project: Year-two evaluation report.* New York: Academy for Educational Development.

Fancsali, C., Nelsestuen, K., & Weinbaum, A. (2001b). *NWP classrooms: Strategies, assignments and student work, National Writing Project evaluation, Year-one results.* New York: Academy for Educational Development.

Fullan, M. (2001). *The new meaning of educational change* (3rd ed.). New York: Teachers College Press.

Fullan, M., & Hargreaves, A. (1996). *What's worth fighting for in your school?* New York: Teachers College Press.

Goodlad, J. I. (1984). *A place called school: Prospects for the future.* New York: McGraw-Hill.

Graves, D. H. (1983). *Writing: Teachers & children at work.* Portsmouth, NH: Heinemann.

Gray, J. (2000). *Teachers at the center: A memoir of the early years of the National Writing Project.* Berkeley, CA: The National Writing Project.

Greene, M. (1978). *Landscapes of learning.* New York: Teachers College Press.

Greene, M. (1995). *Releasing the imagination: Essays on education, the arts, and social change.* San Francisco: Jossey-Bass.

Grossman, P., Wineburg, S., & Woolworth, S. (2000, April). *In pursuit of teacher community.* Paper presented at the annual meeting of the American Educational Research Association, New Orleans.

Grumet, M. R. (1988). *Bitter milk: Women and teaching.* Amherst, MA: University of Massachusetts Press.

Hargreaves, A. (1994). *Changing teachers, changing times: Teachers' work and culture in the postmodern age.* New York: Teachers College Press.

Lave, J., & Wenger, E. (1991). *Situated learning: Legitimate peripheral participation.* Cambridge, UK: Cambridge University Press.

Lieberman, A. (1992). School–university partnerships: A view from the inside. *Kappan, 74*(2), 147–156.

Lieberman, A. (1996). Practices that support teacher development. In M. W. McLaughlin & I. Oberman (Eds.), *Teacher learning* (pp. 185–201). New York: Teachers College Press.

Lieberman, A., & Grolnick, M. (1996). Networks and reform in American education. *Teachers College Record, 98*(1), 8–45.

Lieberman, A., & McLaughlin, M. W. (1992). Networks for educational change: Powerful and problematic. *Kappan, 73*(9), 673–677.

Lieberman, A., & Miller, L. (1991). *Teachers, their world and their work.* New York: Teachers College Press.

Lieberman, A., & Miller, L. (1999). *Teachers transforming their world and their work.* New York: Teachers College Press.

Lieberman, A., & Wood, D. R. (2002). The National Writing Project. *Educational Leadership, 59*(6), 40–43.

Lieberman, A., & Wood, D. R. (in press). The professional development of teachers: Learning in networks. In A. Hargreaves & D. R. Fink (Eds.), *The handbook of leadership and management.* Cambridge, UK: Pearson Press.

Little, J. W. (1993). Teachers' professional development in a climate of educational reform. *Educational Evaluation and Policy Analysis, 15*(2), 129–151.

Little, J. W. (1999). Organizing schools for teacher learning. In L. Darling-Hammond & G. Sykes (Eds.), *Teaching as the learning profession: Handbook of policy and practice* (pp. 233–262). San Francisco: Jossey-Bass.

Lortie, D. (1975). *Schoolteacher: A sociological study.* Chicago: University of Chicago Press.

McDonald, J. (1996). *Redesigning school: Lessons for the 21st century.* San Francisco: Jossey-Bass.

McDonald, J., Hatch, T., Kirby, E., Ames, N., Haynes, M. N., & Joyner, E. (1999). *School reform behind the scenes: How ATLAS is shaping the future of education.* New York: Teachers College Press.

McLaughlin, M. W. (1998). Listening and learning from the field: Tales of policy implementation and situated practice. In A. Hargreaves, A. Lieberman, M. Fullan, & D. Hopkins (Eds.), *The international handbook of educational change* (Part 1, pp. 70–84). Dordrecht, The Netherlands: Kluwer.

McLaughlin, M. W., & Talbert, J. (1993). *Contexts that matter for teaching and learning.* Stanford, CA: Context Center for Secondary School Teaching at Stanford.

McLaughlin, M. W., & Talbert, J. (2001). *Professional communities and the work of high school teaching.* Chicago: University of Chicago Press.

Minnich, E. (1990). *Transforming knowledge.* Philadelphia: Temple University Press.

National Writing Project. (1999). *Fact sheet of the National Writing Project.* Berkeley: University of California.

National Writing Project. (2000). *Annual report of the National Writing Project.* Berkeley: University of California.

Newmann, F., & Wehlage, G. (1995). *Successful school restructuring.* Madison, WI: Center on Organization and Restructuring of Schools.

Parker, A. (1979, October). *Networks for innovation and problem solving and their use for improving education: A comparative review.* Washington, DC: Dissemination Processes Seminar IV.

Schön, D. A. (1983). *The reflective practitioner.* New York: Basic Books.

Smith, F. (1995). *Between hope and havoc: Essays into human learning and education.* Portsmouth, NH: Heinemann.

St. John, M. (1999, November). *A national writing project model: A five-year retrospective on findings from the annual site survey.* (A talk given in November)

St. John, M., Dickey, K., Hirabayashi, J., & Stokes, L., with assistance from Murray, A. (2001, December). *The National Writing Project: Client satisfaction and program impact: Results from a follow-up survey of participants at summer 2000 invitational institutes.* Inverness, CA: Inverness Research Associates.

Sykes, G. (1999). Teacher and student learning: Strengthening the connection. In L. Darling-Hammond & G. Sykes (Eds.), *Teaching as the learning profession: Handbook of policy and practice* (pp. 151–179). San Francisco: Jossey-Bass.

Wenger, E. (1998). *Communities of practice: Learning, meaning, and identity.* Cambridge, UK: Cambridge University Press.

Westheimer, J. (1998). *Among schoolteachers: Community, autonomy, and ideology in teachers' work.* New York: Teachers College Press.

Wineburg, S., & Grossman, P. (1998). Creating a community of learners among high school teachers. *Kappan, 79*(5), 350–353.

Wood, D. R., & Lieberman, A. (2000). Teachers as authors: The National Writing Project's approach to professional development. *International Journal of Leadership in Education, 3*(3), 255–273.

Index

About the Authors

Ann Lieberman is an emeritus professor from Teachers College, Columbia University. She is now a senior scholar at The Carnegie Foundation for the Advancement of Teaching and a visiting professor at Stanford University. She received her M.A. at California State University at Northridge and her Ed.D at the University of California at Los Angeles. Widely known for her work in the areas of teacher leadership and development, collaborative research, networks and school–university partnerships, and problems and prospects for understanding educational change, her work is valued by both researchers and practitioners. Her authored books include *Teachers: Their World and Their Work* and its sequel, *Teachers: Transforming Their World and Their Work* (with Lynne Miller); her edited books include *Building a Professional Culture in Schools* and, most recently, *Teachers Caught in the Action: The Work of Professional Development* (with Lynne Miller). Among her honors and awards, she was president of the American Educational Research Association (AERA) in 1992 and received an honorary doctorate from California State University at Northridge.

Diane R. Wood is an assistant professor in the College of Education and Human Development at the University of Southern Maine. She spent 20 years as a teacher and administrator in high schools, and her present work focuses on professional development of veteran teachers, narrative inquiry as a method for understanding teaching, and democratic change in public school cultures. Her articles have appeared in the *Harvard Educational Review*, *Anthropology and Education Quarterly*, and the *International Journal of Leadership in Education*. She is co-editor of and a contributor to *Transforming Teacher Education: Lessons in Professional Development*.